AGINCOURT

AGINCOURT

Christopher Hibbert

LONDON
B. T. BATSFORD LTD

Military Histories by the same author

WOLFE AT QUEBEC

THE DESTRUCTION OF LORD RAGLAN

CORUNNA

THE BATTLE OF ARNHEM

© Christopher Hibbert, 1964

First published 1964

THIS EDITION PUBLISHED 1978

PRINTED IN GREAT BRITAIN BY
REDWOOD BURN LIMITED, TROWBRIDGE & ESHER
FOR THE PUBLISHERS

B. T. BATSFORD LTD

4 FITZHARDINGE STREET, LONDON W1H 0AH

ISBN 0 7134 1150 3

For F.M.P.,
the Battleaxe

PREFACE

O God, thy arm was here;
And not to us, but to thy arm alone,
Ascribe we all! When, without stratagem,
But in plain shock and even play of battle,
Was ever known so great and little loss
On one part and on th'other? Take it, God,
For it is none but thine!

Whether ascribed to God or to the obsolete tactics and lack of discipline of the French Chivalry, the utter defeat of Charles VI's army at Agincourt on 25 October 1415 was, indeed, astonishing. It was also, a contemporary French chronicler thought, the 'most disgraceful event that had ever happened to the Kingdom of France'.

In this book I have tried to describe not only what happened, but how it happened. In doing so I have been able to draw on the unusual number of contemporary sources with which the historian of this particular campaign in the Hundred Years War is so well supplied. These chronicles are, of course, of varying degrees of authenticity and for this reason—though the book, as all books in the series, is intended for the lay reader rather than the student—I have shown by a small capital letter in the text the source of all the main quotations. I have not, however, attempted to explain the wearisome processes which have resulted in my reconciling conflicting statements in the chronicles, since although the reconciliation has led me to an interpretation of some events different from that reached by previous writers of books on the subject, I can make no claims that I have proved anything. We are all merely guessing and the points at issue are, in any case, only relatively minor ones of time and place.

All the accounts of the campaign in the contemporary chronicles are fairly short and, while I have included in the book every detail that it is possible to glean from them, there inevitably remains much that one would like to know but cannot discover. A fuller treatment could only be made by the elaboration of conjecture.

PREFACE

A note on the chronicles and on the more important of recent sources is given on pages 177-179.

For their help in a variety of ways I want to thank Mrs Joan St George Saunders of Writers' and Speakers' Research, Mrs Peter Crane, Sir Arthur Bryant, Mr Albert Makinson, Mr Jeffrey Herford, Mr Edward Billing, Mr J. W. Rillie, my son, Tom, and my wife.

I want also to thank Mr Peter Kemmis Betty for all his help in the collection of the illustrations.

My much missed mentor at Oxford, the late Captain Cyril Falls, sometime Chichele Professor of the History of War, was kind enough to read the first edition of this book in proof and made several valuable suggestions for its improvement.

CONTENTS

Note—The verses before each chapter are from *The Bataille of Agyncourt* attributed to John Lydgate and from William Shakespeare's *The Life of Henry V*

THE ILLUSTRATIONS

THE ILLUSTRATIONS

Figure

23-4 Henry's helmet and sword *From his Chantry in Westminster Abbey*

25 The King, with a sword *From a mid-fifteenth-century watercolour (B.M. Cotton MS. Julius E. IV)*

26 Henry V on horseback *From the counterseal of the Gold Seal of Henry V, 1415*

27 Henry at the siege of Caen, 1417 *From the 'Life and Acts of Richard Beauchamp, Earl of Warwick' (op. cit.)*

28 The marriage of Henry V and Catherine of Valois, daughter of Charles VI *From the 'Life and Acts of Richard Beauchamp, Earl of Warwick' (op. cit.)*

Note—In some of the plates in this book the men-at-arms appear in armour of the artist's time rather than that of the scene depicted. By 1415 most of the knights were wearing complete plate armour (though less developed than that portrayed in the later illustrations), but some of the less wealthy knights and other ranks still retained the mail aventail (shown in the earlier illuminations), which hung down from the bascinet to protect the neck. This difference is clear in the line illustrations on page 34, which are both taken from church brasses of 1415.

ACKNOWLEDGMENT

Figure 3 is reproduced by gracious permission of Her Majesty the Queen.

The Author and Publishers wish to thank the following for permission to reproduce the illustrations appearing in this book: -

The Trustees of the British Museum for figs 2, 4, 5, 10, 13, 14, 17, 18, 21, 22 and 25-28

Photo Bulloz for figs 15 and 20

His Grace the Archbishop of Canterbury and the Trustees of the Lambeth Palace Library for fig 19

Giraudon for figs 11 and 16

E. C. Le Grice for fig 12

A. W. Kerr, F.I.B.P., F.R.P.S., for fig 6

Ministry of Public Building and Works for fig 9

Royal Commission on Historical Monuments for figs 3 and 7

E. A. Sollars for fig 8

The Trustees of the Victoria and Albert Museum for the line illustrations on pages 34, 97, 125

The Dean and Chapter of Westminster Abbey for figs 23 and 24.

This story shall the good man teach his son;
And Crispin Crispian shall ne'er go by,
From this day to the ending of the world,
But we in it shall be remembered.

King Henry V, Act IV, Sc. iii

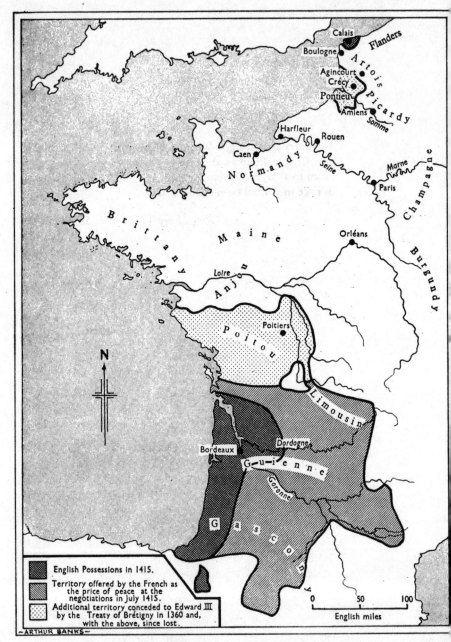

Calais
Boulogne
Flanders
Agincourt
Crécy
Artois
Picardy
Pontieu
Amiens
Somme
Harfleur
Rouen
Caen
Normandy
Seine
Marne
Paris
Champagne
Brittany
Maine
Orléans
Burgundy
Loire
Anjou
Poitou
Poitiers
Limousin
Dordogne
Bordeaux
Guienne
Garonne
Gascony

N

English Possessions in 1415.
Territory offered by the French as the price of peace at the negotiations in July 1415.
Additional territory conceded to Edward III by the Treaty of Brétigny in 1360 and, with the above, since lost.

0   50   100
English miles

~ARTHUR BANKS~

English possessions in France in 1415

Prologue

Our Kyng ordeyned with all his myght
For to amende that is amys,
And that is all for Engelond ryght,
To geten agen that scholde it ben his;
That is, al Normandie forsothe y wys,
By right of eritage he scholde it have,
Thereof he seith he wyll nought mys,
Crist kepe his body sounde and save.
      Wot ye right well that thus it was.
      Gloria tibi trinitas!

⚜

Now are we well resolved; and, by God's help,
And yours, the noble sinews of our power,
France being ours, we'll bend it to our awe,
Or break it all to pieces: or there we'll sit,
Ruling in large and ample empery
O'er France and all her almost kingly dukedoms,
Or lay these bones in an unworthy urn,
Tombless, with no remembrance over them:

I

On Passion Sunday, 1413, while snow and sleet fell through the cold wind outside, Henry V was crowned in Westminster Abbey. He was twenty-five. Three weeks before he had kissed his dying father for the last time in the Abbot's house near by and had taken up the iron Lancastrian crown that was his dangerous inheritance. The responsibilities it imposed upon him already seemed to have changed his character. The gay, even foppish, youth had become a grave and thoughtful man. On the evening of his father's death he had gone away by himself to think and to pray; and now as he was anointed with the miraculous oil of St Thomas of Canterbury his devout and humble behaviour impressed all who saw him.

He was considered a handsome man, though the long and prominent nose, the thin eyebrows, the high smooth brow, the very red and tightly compressed lips and the heavy, lantern jaw are features no longer admired. The back of his neck and the sides of his head were shaved, as the heads of soldiers were, so that his hair, thick, brown and uncurled, looked like a round fur cap. His ears were small and shapely, his teeth even and very white, his large hazel eyes clear and bright. He seemed, despite his solemnity, to be very much alive. Men looked at him and could find grounds for hope that his father's reign, which had opened with usurpation, rebellion, plague and persecution and had ended in fear, lassitude and gloom, would be followed by a new age, as brilliant and adventurous as that of the young King's great-grandfather, Edward III.

It was this King Edward who, sixty-seven years before, had won his great victory over the French at Crécy and ten years later his son, the Black Prince, had defeated them again at Poitiers. And it was to Edward III that Henry V, as well as his people, looked back in pride and admiration.

The series of wars that Edward had begun in 1337—the wars that historians were later to term the Hundred Years War—were the outcome of a quarrel that had been festering for a long time. The quarrel had been inevitable if not ever since William, Duke of Normandy, a vassal of the King of France, had become King of England, certainly ever since the uneasy and complicated feudal relationships between the two kings had been further aggravated by the marriage of William's great-grandson, Henry II, to Eleanor, the divorced wife of Louis VII. Henry, who was already Count of Anjou, acquired through his wife the additional territories of Poitou, Guienne and Gascony and so allied to the English crown, dominions in France that rivalled the possessions of the French King himself who yet was still, in feudal theory, Henry's overlord.

By the time of Edward II's death these vast territories had been greatly reduced but the successful campaigns of his son Edward III had almost restored the balance. By the Treaty of Brétigny (1360) Edward III had gained much of what he had fought for—absolute control of great territories in the south-west that stretched almost from the Loire to the Pyrenees, and in the north Calais and Ponthieu (see figure 1). Since then English fortunes had steadily declined. Edward III had drooped into dotage. His gifted son the Black Prince fell ill and died; while Charles V of France, helped by his brother Philip the Bold, Duke of Burgundy and by his highly gifted Fabian general, Bertrand Duguesclin, advanced to take back much of what their enemies had lately won. By 1375 the English had been pushed back into Calais and to strips of land round Bordeaux and the harbours of Brittany. And as the fourteenth century ended, the war died away in a series of indecisive raids and expeditions.

Edward III's successor, Richard II, did not want to renew it at all, and Henry IV could not renew it with force. But Henry V soon showed himself determined to do so. Both the time and the mood of his people favoured him.

⚜

King Charles V of France had died in 1380. His brother, Philip the Bold, had lived on for a further twenty-four years. But Philip's death in 1404 had left Charles's son and successor, King Charles VI, without the support he so badly needed. Charles VI was only forty-four when Henry V became King of England but, plagued by a detested wife who flaunted her lovers in his face, he was already prematurely old and intermittently mad, one of his convictions being that he was made of glass and that if people came too near him he would break.

As well as being ruled by a sadly unstable King, France, although at the beginning of the century the strongest and most prosperous power in Europe, was now being torn apart by rivalries, resentments and jealousies. Philip the Bold's son, John, the new Duke of Burgundy, whose dominion included not only Burgundy itself, but immense tracts of land in northern France and what are now Belgium and Holland, had violently quarrelled with his cousin, Louis, Duke of Orléans, who, as the younger son of Charles V, had formidable power in central and southern France. In 1407 the Duke of Orléans was murdered by agents of the Duke of Burgundy and the feuds which followed this terrible culmination of their quarrel crippled France for years to come and were an even greater encouragement to an English invasion than the incapacity of her demented King.

⚜

Soon after his accession Henry revived the claims of his ancestors. He demanded the return of territories that had been granted to Edward III at the Treaty of Brétigny and was later to revive Edward III's claim to the French crown, maintaining that it was his by right of succession from his great-great-grandmother Isabella, daughter of Philip IV.* His aims were set forth by one of the priests of his chapel: 'Those things that make for the honour of God, the extension of the Church, the freeing of his country, and the tranquility of Kingdoms, and especially of the two kingdoms of England and France which, from long and unhappy times past had damaged each other and caused deplorable effusion of human blood.' [A]

In realising these ambitions, Henry was anxious to obtain the support of the devious and equivocal Duke of Burgundy whose dominions in Flanders and consequent concern for the maintenance of the English wool trade might make him a more reliable ally, or at

* A genealogical table, showing the relationship between the English and the French kings, is given in Appendix I.

least a more reliable neutral, than he could otherwise have been expected to be. Negotiations were accordingly opened in an effort to discover grounds for mutual help. Just as Henry had need of the Duke of Burgundy's friendship, so the Duke had need of his, for since the murder of the Duke of Orléans, three other royal dukes, Berry, Bourbon and Brittany, and Bernard, Count of Armagnac, had all drawn closer round the Orleanist cause.

While secretly negotiating with the Duke of Burgundy, Henry was at the same time openly negotiating with representatives of the rival Orleanists, hoping, no doubt, to increase the price of his friendship. He was also proposing marriage to King Charles's daughter, Catherine. But neither the French nor the English diplomats seem ever to have expected their talks to result in a treaty satisfactory to both sides; and it appeared, indeed, that the English King did not even want them to be, for as the negotiations proceeded his demands increased until they went far beyond what a reversion to the terms of the Treaty of Brétigny would have given him. Certainly by the autumn of 1414, though the negotiations were still going on, Henry was preparing actively for war.

Henry's shield

Preparation

Now all the youth of England are on fire,
And silken dalliance in the wardrobe lies:
Now thrive the armorers, and honour's thought
Reigns solely in the breast of every man:
They sell the pasture now to buy the horse,
Following the mirror of all Christian kings,
With winged heels, as English Mercuries.
For now sits Expectation in the air,
And hides a sword from hilts unto the point
With crowns imperial, crowns and coronets,
Promised to Harry and his followers.
The French, advised by good intelligence
Of this most dreadful preparation,
Shake in their fear and with pale policy
Seek to divert the English purposes.

2

The preparations raised little protest. War was not unpopular. The campaigns of Edward III had been extremely expensive, but, because of the demands for money which the King had had to make, Parliament could congratulate itself on its importance and growing indispensability; while the taxes which were levied for military expeditions fell most heavily on those classes who might reimburse themselves from the profits that war brought. Nor could it be said that there were no financial returns for those who did not make money directly out of war, since the pay and bonuses, the ransom money and the valuable plunder which the fighting man brought back with him were profits that were eventually shared with the classes that stayed at home. Also there was hope that the cost of war would to some extent be offset by the revenues of conquered territories.

Farsighted men might have envisaged the sort of moral problems that war, particularly so long a war, might be expected to arouse, and the problems of returning soldiers unable or unwilling to settle down to peaceable and honest pursuits. But these were not immediate problems and their impact lay in the future, years after the Hundred Years War had stumbled at last to its close, when the Wars of the Roses were bringing the Middle Ages themselves to an end.

For those who were to fight in the war in France there was adventure to be had as well as profit and, although the army had become a professional one, adventure and the opportunity to excel in the most dangerous sport of all were still the principal lures for many of those who joined it. 'Prowess', Froissart had written towards the end of the previous century, and his contention still held good, 'Prowess is so noble a virtue that one must never pass over it too briefly, for it is the mother stuff and the light of noble men and, as the log cannot spring to life without fire, so the noble man cannot come to perfect honour or to the glory of the world without prowess.'

France had long provided the upper classes with a military training ground far more thrilling than the marches of Wales and Scotland; but the sort of warfare that had recently been carried on there had been devoid of all but passing interest and intermittent pleasure and had served only to give England's war leaders a taste for campaigning and a desire for more profitable and exciting action. To fight a full-scale war, to transfer the tournament from the lists to the battlefield, to indulge a passion for aggressive tests of skill against worthy opponents—these were ambitions that burned in the heart of every true knight. There was, too, something pleasurable in the thought of fighting and killing Frenchmen. For the English regarded the French with that mixture of reluctant admiration, envy and frustration that five-and-a-half centuries have done little to change. French nobles were masters of the techniques of chivalry and of courtly love; and although the English nobleman spoke French and had far more in common with the French nobleman, with whom his ties of blood and birth and interest so closely linked him, than with the English merchant now rising to an affluence as great as his own, he saw in the opportunity of defeating him a challenge to his skill, his strength and his virility.

The poorer classes did not, of course, share these mutual interests and rivalries. So far as they were concerned the French had been enemies of England for most of the past half-century and since Poitiers no victory over them had caught their imagination or filled them with pride. Indeed, in recent years it seemed that the French had been having things all their own way. Certainly they had several times raided the coast more or less with impunity. Plymouth had been burned by French marauders in 1403; in 1404 the Isle of Wight had been invaded; and in the following year a French force had landed at Milford Haven to give support to the Welsh rebels. Indignation at past insults such as these—though news of them was, of course, slow to spread—was now aggravated by what the people took to be French duplicity during the negotiations which their young King was so patiently conducting. Accusations of guile have subsequently been more often levelled against the English negotiators than the French, but at the time it could be made to appear that if the talks broke down the French would be entirely responsible. When, therefore, the English envoys returned from France for the last time without a settlement, the people were satisfied that war was justified; and the rumour that the mission had returned with a present of tennis-balls for Henry and a suggestion that he should play with them like a good boy instead of meddling with matters beyond his capacity made war seem not merely justified but essential. The rumour had little foundation and the tennis-balls almost certainly did not arrive in England, even if some insolent French knight did suggest that they should be sent; but it was the sort of story that inflames war fever, and nothing was done to deny it.

By the time of the mission's return preparations for war were well advanced. Already the previous winter, in November 1414, the Chancellor, Bishop Beaufort of Winchester, had addressed a Parliament summoned by Henry and told its members in a long and pedantic speech that the King 'deemed that the proper time had arrived for the accomplishment of his purpose'. Three things were needed, the Bishop said: 'wise and faithful counsel from the King's vassals; strong and true support from his people; and a copious subsidy from his subjects'. And all of them, the Bishop did not doubt, would be granted, 'because the more their King's dominions were extended, the less would their burthens become; and these things being performed, great honour and glory would necessarily ensue'.

The speech had its required effect. Although they discreetly suggested, as they had done before, that no 'voyage' should be undertaken before the resources of diplomacy had been exhausted and cautiously limited its use to the 'defence of the Kingdom and the safety of the seas', the Commons voted a subsidy generous enough to make an invasion possible.

Generous as it was, however, it was far from enough to make possible an invasion as ambitious as Henry had in mind; and he found it necessary to send Commissioners all over the country to borrow money wherever they could, often making it clear, particularly to foreign merchants, that the loans were not entirely optional. Within the next seven years large sums were raised in this way to be repaid with money derived from taxation, customs and other government income. The City of London, for example, lent over £32,000, religious orders nearly £9,000, the staff of the Exchequer £2,474 and the bishops—in order, so it was afterwards alleged, to encourage the King to go abroad and thus render a feared attack on Church property unlikely—lent no less than £44,243. Many private citizens contributed and the name of Richard Whittington appears in the records as having lent £2,000. No interest was paid on the loans but nearly all of them were eventually repaid, though few in full.

The great number of loans were necessary, for war had already become an immensely expensive business. Not only enormous quantities of arrows and bowstaves, cords and feathers, had to be paid for, not only guns and gunpowder, not only pontoons, scaling ladders, battering rams, wagons, provisions, horseshoes, tools, equipment and weapons of all kinds, but a huge fleet had to be assembled and measures had to be taken to ensure its uninterrupted passage across the Channel.

The ships used in later expeditions had not yet been built and, although many of the vessels collected for the 1415 expedition were forcibly seized without compensation, and some were supplied by the Cinque Ports in accordance with their charters, many others had to be hired, several of them in Holland. There were, in addition, the wages of the men who sailed the ships and of the soldiers who served in the bigger ones as marines. These soldiers, it appears from a surviving account, were paid at the same rate as they would have been paid on land, and this was a much more generous rate than the sailors received. Even the masters of ships had only 6d. a day, the sum allowed to the ships' archers; and the ordinary sailors, nearly all of whom were pressed, had no more than 3d. a day plus a bounty of 6d. a week. But, although the wages were small, the numbers to be paid were very great, for an average barge of a hundred tons required a crew of forty-eight, and when all the ships were finally assembled in the Solent there were no less than 1,500 craft of various types and tonnage.

The by now usual method of raising the army that was to sail in these ships was also expensive—far more so than the methods of earlier times.

The King still had the constitutional right to demand military service from his subjects; and in former centuries he had done so,

PREPARATION

both by calling out the feudal levy, and by issuing Commissions of
Array to the leading gentry of the shires to assemble a militia.
The unit of feudal land-tenure was the knight's fee and the man
who held such a fee was in duty bound to serve the king in the field
for forty days in every year. Landowners who held a number of
knight's fees—some held several hundreds—had to provide the
requisite number of deputies. Theoretically, then, the King could
always call upon a substantial body of cavalry to fight for him. In
practice, however, the feudal host, often ill-disciplined and reluc-
tantly assembled, was far from being an efficient fighting force even
in the shortest campaign, and for campaigns which lasted longer
than forty days it was frequently impossible to maintain an adequate
force at all, even when payment was made. The troops assembled in
the shires by Commissions of Array were as open to criticism as the
feudal levies and could not, in any case, be forced to go on foreign
expeditions.

Various attempts to improve and extend the military resources of
the country had been made from time to time. By the Assize of Arms
of 1181 Henry II had stipulated the weapons and armour that those
called upon to serve him should possess; and a hundred years later
Edward I had confirmed these obligations in the Statute of Winchester which divided fighting men into five classes, each knight, as
one of the upper class, being expected to provide himself with at
least a full suit of armour and a helmet, a sword, a knife and a horse,
and every man in the fifth class, however poor, being expected to
possess a bow and a quiverful of arrows. But while the strength of
cavalry could to some extent be increased by compelling landowners
with estates worth more than twenty pounds a year to take on
knighthood or pay a very heavy fine, no such means were available
for increasing the strength of the King's infantry; and distraint of
knighthood itself was in any case fiercely resisted. It had, therefore, been necessary to have recourse to foreign mercenaries.

If Magna Carta were to be respected, however, Edward I could
not rely to any important extent on foreign troops to make up the
large gaps in his army. And he had accordingly been obliged to
develop and extend the system of payment by granting regular
wages to all his English soldiers as well as paying annuities to
knights in return for their service when summoned. The method

was extremely expensive in a mediaeval economy and contributed an added burden to the cost of an ambitious expedition which could now account for over half the King's annual revenue. It did, though, enable an army based on voluntary enlistment to develop and it did provide a nucleus of trained professional troops.

The system of payment had been developed throughout the fourteenth century and by the fifteenth it had become common practice to raise an army by contract. The contracts were placed with various leading soldiers—only a few of them foreigners—who undertook to enlist an agreed number of men-at-arms (that is to say knights and esquires who fought, either mounted or on foot, in full armour) and an agreed number of archers, for a certain period and to bring them together at a muster supervised by officials of the Exchequer, '*bien montez, armez et araiez comme a leur estatz ils appartient*'.

The king was not usually held liable for the first instalment of wages, which were paid by the contracting noble, knight or esquire who in return received security and pledges that he would be reimbursed by the Exchequer when he presented his men at the muster or as soon afterwards as the king could afford it. The king also guaranteed that he would provide transport, both on the outward journey and coming home, for each contracting officer, his retinue, baggage and horses.

Transport for the horses was a particularly important consideration as the numbers usually taken were immense. A duke was allowed fifty for his own use, an earl twenty-four, a knight six, an esquire four and a horse archer one. The specialist troops, tradesmen and clerks also took horses with them, and there were in addition hundreds of pack animals. Perhaps as many as 25,000 horses sailed with the 1415 expedition.

The division of ransoms, like the number of horses, was another matter for agreement between the king and the contracting officer. Prisoners of war were extremely valuable commodities—the French King John who was captured at Poitiers had been held to ransom for three million gold crowns and it has been estimated by Edouard Perroy that Edward III received as much as £268,000 in ransom money between 1360 and 1370. The expenses of war could, therefore, to a large extent be reduced by selling prisoners back to their families.

Each prisoner theoretically belonged to the man who captured him, but the profits derived from his disposal had to be shared. Usually the captor received only a fraction of the money paid, a large proportion going to the noble or knight under whose banner he served and this leader in turn had to divide his share with the king. Certain men, if captured, had to be handed over to the king anyway; and in the 1415 expedition the 'Adversary of France, or any of his sons, nephews, uncles, or cousins, or any King of any Kingdom or his lieutenant, or other chieftains having command from the said Adversary of France' were all reserved in this way. Similar arrangements applied to the division of booty or 'gagnes of war'.*

Obviously a man without considerable resources could not afford to enter into a contract with the king, certainly not if he were to hold himself liable for the payment of a large retinue for an uncertain period. The King's brother, the Duke of Clarence, for instance, who agreed to provide 240 men-at-arms and 720 horse archers for the 1415 campaign, had a weekly wages bill of over £250. It was inevitable that men faced with payments on this scale would demand immediate and adequate security as well as Letters of Protection exempting them from civil processes and losses incurred in consequence of the expedition; and the provision of satisfactory security, as in previous reigns, presented the king with a problem he could solve in only one way—by pledging his most valuable possessions.

Henry, in fact, pawned all his crown jewels and when these had been committed he offered his silver and even the vestments and reliquaries of his chapel. Several of his crowns were pawned, and one at least, which was to be redeemed by the Feast of the Circumcision, 1416, 'whole and without damage and injury', was temporarily broken up so that pieces of it could be distributed as pledges to those who required them.

⚜

Henry had already learned, during the campaigns he had been on as a young man in Wales against the rebel leader Owen Glyn Dŵr, the

* One contract (made between Henry V and Thomas Tunstall, Esquire, on 29 April 1415) incorporating most of the usual provisions is printed in Appendix II.

value of making arrangements for the payment of wages punctually and regularly on a set scale to apply throughout the army. And in April 1415 he announced the scales that would apply in the forthcoming campaign; and the amount of bonuses that were to be paid to those leaders who brought more than thirty men to the muster. Dukes—all dukes at this time were royal dukes—were to receive 13s. 4d. a day, earls 6s. 8d. a day, barons 4s., knights 2s., other men-at-arms 1s., and archers, whether they had horses or not, 6d. In addition to these fighting troops—about 2,000 knights and men-at-arms and 8,000 archers were eventually mustered—there were great numbers of pages, grooms, guides, hobelars (the light horsemen whose mounts wore no armour) acting as messengers, carters, tradesmen and specialists of all sorts, for an army was already by the beginning of the fifteenth century a far more complicated and technical organisation than it is usually presented as having been. There were smiths and armourers, painters and tent-makers, fletchers and bowyers, turners and carpenters, masons, wheelwrights, cordeners, saddlers, purveyors, quartermasters and farriers.* Apart from the surgeons, the chaplains, the legal and clerical staff, and the trumpeters and pipers, there were numerous officials from the various departments of the Royal Household—the Chamber, the Wardrobe, the Hall, the Poultry, the Bakehouse, the Kitchen, the Pantry, the Scullery, the Buttery, the Napery, the Spicery. There were also three heralds, Leicester, Guienne and Ireland, whose duties included the carrying of formal messages and challenges, and the supervision of rules of precedence and etiquette, to be observed not only in camp but in dealing with enemy leaders, during truces or after surrender.

These heralds were necessary, for war was still overlaid with all the trappings of chivalry despite the presence in the King's retinue of 120 miners and seventy-five gunners, led by four Master Gunners, all Dutchmen. Indeed, the use of artillery, though now accepted as essential by most military commanders and, in particular, by the King himself, was still thought by the more conservative to be an unwarrantable interference with the traditional and chivalrous conduct of war and its former niceties.

But although artillery was beginning to take some of the social

* Most of these men were attached to the King's retinue which was in itself an immense headquarters, as can be seen in Appendix III.

privileges out of warfare—since a flying gunstone was just as dangerous to a knight in armour as to an archer in a cloth coat, and a gunner was, in any case, by no means a gentleman—there was otherwise little less social distinction in the army than there had always been.

A knight went on board with his servants and grooms, sometimes even with his chaplain, and with rarely less than the six horses he was allowed. His armour and heavy weapons were carried for him by an apprentice with aspirations to knighthood himself and this young man helped his master to put his armour on whenever it was required. This, of course, was a laborious and skilled process for each piece of the harness had to be put on in a certain way and at a certain time, and if one piece went on in the wrong order it might not be possible to put on the others. The reticulated steel shoes, for example, had to go on before the leg guards which fitted over the ankle. Mail was easier to put on, of course, but mail, which was excessively heavy and could be knocked into the flesh by a particularly heavy blow with a poleaxe, had been virtually abandoned by now in favour of steel plate.

In battle the whole body was encased in steel plate with gussets of mail used only to fill up the joints in various places and as an extra protection round the neck between the back and breast plates and the helmet. The helmet worn in battle—more properly known as a bascinet since the crested helmet was normally reserved for the lists —fitted closely round the head but left much of the face exposed, so that a detachable nosepiece or visor was fitted to afford as much protection as could be combined with reasonable vision. The full suit when worn with all its attachments, with its pauldrons that overlapped the shoulder reticulations and its circular palletes that protected the armpits and elbow joints, its lance rest and knee guards, was, naturally, extremely heavy, though it did not prevent a strong man moving about in it with agility.

On top of his armour the knight wore his *côte d'armes*, a loose emblazoned coat, sometimes short like a tabard, sometimes with a trailing back, and his baudrick or ornamented sword belt tied round his hips. His hands were usually encased in inner gloves of velvet and outer gauntlets of hardened leather with overlapping steel plates and spikes of iron, called gadlings, on his knuckles.

Knightly armour at the time of Agincourt
From church brasses of c. 1415

Fitting all these pieces of steel plate, attachments and accessories round the body of his master and fitting his master's horse with its mail and emblazoned caparison naturally took the apprentice and groom a long time; but as surprising the enemy was unthinkable to the truly chivalrous spirit, there was little danger attached to the delay.

Apart from their swords and daggers and lances, most knights possessed an axe and one or more of a variety of heavy bludgeoning weapons; and it was, indeed, these which they frequently found most useful. For in battle there were few opportunities for the exercise of skilled swordsmanship, since great strength, stamina and courageous determination were attributes more likely to gain the victory in what was usually a confused *mêlée*.

❧

The archer, unlike the man-at-arms, was always more or less ready for battle. His protective clothing—if, indeed, he wore any at all—was often limited to a leather jacket which sometimes, like those worn by cross-bowmen, had plates of iron on the breast and at the elbows. A few archers, usually those who were mounted, had chain hauberks and the black cloth jackets of others were lined with mail, but for the most part those who took part in the 1415 expedition were without metal armour. They were also for the most part, it seems, without the steel or chain skull cap worn on previous campaigns and wore instead conical hats made of boiled leather or tarpaulin-covered wickerwork strengthened inside with strips of iron, though these, apparently, were far from universal.

They all, however, wore belts in which they stuck their swords and lead mallets and axes or whatever other weapons they carried in addition to their bows. Their arrows were often also stuck through their belts as they did not all have quivers. These arrows, which were about three feet long, had sharp tips of steel—capable of penetrating through an oak door four inches thick—smooth wooden shafts, and flights of duck or peacock feathers or, more rarely, of parchment. The bows were about five feet long and the best of them were made of yew, though, to prevent too many yew trees being cut down for this purpose, bowyers were instructed from time to time to make four bows of wych-hazel, ash, or elm to every one they made of yew. The bowstring was drawn back to the ear, unlike the string of the short-bow arrow which was drawn back only to the chest, and a skilled long-bowman could shoot accurately at distances up to 300 yards.

This formidable skill was not easily acquired and the archer practised constantly. Ever since Henry I had discovered that the charge of even the most heavily armoured cavalrymen could be weakened by a hail of well-directed arrows, the bowman had, in fact, been encouraged to do so by a succession of ordinances, one of which decreed that if an archer killed a man while practising, the misadventure should not be considered a crime, and another—passed for the first time in 1363 and subsequently re-enacted—that prohibited all other sports on Sundays and Feast Days.

For years after Hastings the short-bow had remained the usual weapon of the English archer, although on the Continent the more complicated but more efficient cross-bow had been in use since the tenth century. The English, however, had never taken to the cross-bow, despite its proved worth during the Crusades, and had always associated it with mercenaries like the Genoese archers who were, indeed, its most skilled users. And it was not until the archers of South Wales showed Edward I the range and power of the long-bow that this became the principal weapon of English infantry. By becoming so it had revolutionised both the organisation and tactics of the English army. Edward I's army on the Continent in 1297 had contained 7,810 infantry, three-quarters of them Welsh, and only 895 cavalry. Edward III's army contained a higher proportion of cavalry, but not of knights, for the additional mounted men were horse-archers who could pursue the retreating enemy at great speed after his cavalry attack had been stopped and broken by the line of armoured knights and foot-archers.

The officers still all came from the knightly classes, of course, and the archers were always placed under the command of particular men-at-arms. The men-at-arms themselves—though circumstances of social rank and the size of retinues often altered the system in practice—were theoretically divided up into groups of between twenty-five and eighty men usually commanded by an experienced knight. Two or more of these groups formed larger organisational groups (normally about two hundred men) known as banners which were commanded by bannerets, a rank originally conferred only upon those who could bring a certain number of men into the field and roughly equivalent to the present-day battalion commander.

But, although the social distinction between archer and man-at-arms was still sharply defined, the distinction was not as sharp as it was in the French army where knights had been known to refuse to serve with socially inferior infantrymen; nor did it lead the English man-at-arms to deny the difference the archer and the long-bow had made to his own military position. The reputation of the long-bow, established at Falkirk and increased by the victories at Crécy and Poitiers had, in fact, now become unassailable. And those who used it with such effect, the 'stout yeomen' of England—a stock that was to remain associated with all that was best in English life—were acknowledged the finest infantry in Europe.

⚜

While these archers were being collected together from villages and market towns in Wales as well as England, preparations for war continued apace.

Since the summer of 1413 smiths had been at work on siege guns at Bristol and in the Tower; and on 22 September 1414 Nicholas Merbury, 'Master of the King's works, guns and other ordnance', received orders to find more smiths and labourers for the further guns that would be needed. Four days later the export of gunpowder was prohibited.

On 11 April 1415 Nicholas Mauduyt, sergeant-at-arms, was told to arrest all ships carrying twenty tons or more 'as well belonging to this Kingdom as to other Countries, which were then in the river Thames, and in other sea ports of the realm, as far as Newcastle-upon-Tyne, or which might arrive there before the 1st of May; and the said vessels were to be at the ports of Southampton, London, or Winchelsea by the 8th May at the latest.' Orders were also issued for the ships that Richard Clyderowe and Simon Flete had hired in Holland to be brought to the same ports and to Sandwich, while the masters of all ships were authorised to impress sailors.

At the same time writs were directed to Nicholas Frost, Bowyer, to provide, at the King's charge, workmen to make and repair bows and to collect wood from any place he liked except from land belonging to the Church; to Robert Hunt, Sergeant of the Wagons of the Household, to provide carpenters, wheelwrights and smiths, as well as materials to make carts; to Stephen Ferrour, Sergeant of the King's Farriers, to provide smiths and iron for horseshoes; to Simon Lewys and John Benet, Masons, to provide one hundred masons; to John Southmede, Cartwright, to provide sixty-two carts complete with harness, halters and collars; to Thomas Mathews and

William Gille to provide 120 carpenters and turners; to William Mersh and Nicholas Shokyngton to provide forty smiths. Sheriffs of various counties were ordered to levy cattle and to make arrangements for the brewing of ale and the baking of bread, for until the army could live on the resources of the country in France, sufficient food and drink had to be made available for the men to buy out of their wages.

Arrangements were also made for the security of the country while the King and his army were away. The principal knights and esquires of each county were ordered to take a review of all men-at-arms who would not be leaving with the expedition and of all others capable of bearing arms and to keep them in readiness for home protection. A nightly watch was provided for in every town and no tavern-keeper was to allow any unknown person to remain under his roof for more than one day and one night without know-ledge of the cause of his stay. If the stranger refused to divulge the reason, he was to be arrested and imprisoned.

On 16 April 1415, Bishop Beaufort, the Chancellor, told a meeting of the Council at Westminster that the King had 'undertaken' to go on his voyage. The following day, the King's brother, the Duke of Bedford, was appointed Lieutenant of England during the King's absence and a Council of Defence was appointed for the safeguarding of the Welsh and Scottish frontiers and the Calais Pale.

But although the decision to go to war had been taken and announced, negotiations with the threatened enemy still continued. The last English diplomatic mission returned in June 1415 having settled nothing. Arrangements had been made, nevertheless, for the reception of another French mission in England the following month. The French left Paris prepared to compromise. But Henry awaited their arrival determined to concede nothing. There could be no doubt now that he was determined to fight, not only so as to triumph by force but also to 'busy restless minds in foreign quarrels'. The talks would, however, provide him with a platform on which to proclaim the justice of his cause.

He had already insisted upon its justice and the reluctance with which he contemplated using force to achieve it in letters to the French King which have, understandably, driven nineteenth-century historians to shocked protest. 'Henry may have believed in the justice of his claims', Sir James Ramsay wrote, 'but to call on Heaven to witness his desire for peace was nothing short of blasphemous hypocrisy.' Later writers, hardened, perhaps, in a more cynical school and less ready to condemn the necessary evasions and distortions of diplomatic activity, have not been so harsh. The letters, all the same, do sound a note which even by mediaeval standards sounds both patronising and hypocritical and which cannot be completely muffled by excuse.

Henry, styling himself by the grace of God 'King of England and of France', had addressed his first letter to the 'most serene Prince, Charles, by the Grace of God our very dear cousin', on 4 April 1415. 'We have endeavoured from our accession to our crown', he told him, 'from the ardent passion that we have had for the love of Him who is the author of peace to reconcile the differences between us and our people, to chase and banish for ever that sad division, mother of so many misfortunes, cause of the misery of so many men, and of the loss of so many souls which have been shipwrecked in the slaughter of war.' He protested 'before God and all men' that he himself earnestly desired peace and he reminded Charles that 'we shall have to answer before God for that we retain by force which rightly belongs to another'.

In the second letter, written a week later, Henry returned to the same theme. 'We shall propose nothing to you', he assured Charles, 'which we have not a right conscientiously to demand; and we advise you most Serene Prince, with all sincerity and from pure love, to entertain those happy thoughts of peace which you have always observed from your most tender youth, and not to neglect or abandon them in so mature and advanced an age'—Charles was still only forty-six—'Reflect upon the years which you have passed. Think of eternity.'

When the French delegation arrived in England in July, Henry repeated this advice to Guillaume Boisratier, Archbishop of Bourges, who headed it. The Archbishop replied that his sovereign, King Charles, was willing to submit to the judgment of Christendom 'whether he had not always wished for peace, and whether he had not sought it by all just and honourable means; in proof of which he was willing to dismember his Kingdom by ceding to England many important territories and towns, and to give Henry his daughter Catherine in marriage with 800,000 gold crowns, a dowry which was unprecedented.'

Later on in the discussions, which even at this stage were carried on with the extreme formality of contemporary ambassadorial etiquette, the French delegation offered an even larger dowry and even greater territorial concessions; but Henry was not to be satisfied. All his claims were just, he continued to insist, and Charles VI would be responsible for a 'deluge of Christian blood' if they were not fully met.

'Sir, the King of France, our Sovereign Lord, is the true King of France', the Archbishop spiritedly replied according to one chronicler, 'and with respect to those things to which you say you have a right, you have no lordship, not even to the Kingdom of England, which belongs to the true heirs of the late King Richard. Nor with you can our Sovereign Lord safely treat.'

The discussions were at an end. In a 'haughty tone' Henry told the French mission to depart and said that he would 'quickly follow them'. Before doing so, however, he was careful not to miss an opportunity of exercising his talent for making righteous indignation a basis for propaganda. He sent off to the Emperor Sigismund and 'other Catholic princes', who might be expected to share his constantly reiterated concern for Christian unity, a memorandum setting out his version of the whole history of his quarrel, 'to the effect that all the world might know what wrongs the duplicity of the French had inflicted on him, and that he was being compelled, unwillingly and involuntarily, to raise his standard against the rebels'. [A] A few days later he wrote to Charles for the last time, exhorting him 'in the name of the merciful bowels of Jesus Christ to do us justice'.

Henry wrote from Southampton. In a fortnight the fleet would be ready to sail.

Departure

'I warne you,' he seyde, 'both olde and younge,
Make you redy withoughte delay;
At Southampton to mete youre Kynge,
At Lammas on Seynt Petrys day,
By the Grace of God ant Swete Mary,
Over the see y-thenke to passe'.
The Kyng let ordeyn soue in hy,
What y mene ye knowe the casse.
    Wot ye right well that thus it was.
    Gloria tibi trinitas!

⚜

Then forth, dear countrymen: let us deliver
Our puissance into the hand of God,
Putting it straight in expedition.
Cheerly to sea; the signs of war advance:
No king of England, if not king of France.

3

For miles along the Hampshire coast opposite the Isle of Wight, every inlet and creek was filled with shipping. At anchor off Spithead was the *Trinité Royale*, the King's flagship and the finest ship in his navy. Flying above the masthead was the *Trinité's* banner woven with representations of the three persons of the Godhead and Our Lady and the arms of St Edward, St George and England. The topcastle was surmounted with a crown of burnished copper-gilt; on the capstan was a sceptre wrought with three *fleurs-de-lys* and at the deckhead a leopard carved in gold-painted wood, wearing a silver crown. Her master, Stephen Thomas, had a crew of 300. She was the biggest of the King's ships, with a portage of 500 tons.

Around the *Trinité Royale* and the King's other ships—the *Katherine de la Toure*, the *Petite Trinité de la Toure* and the *Rude Coq de la Toure*—and as far as the eye could stretch up the roadstead and east and west along the Solent were ships of every sort and size, their red waists decked with strange serpents, their bulwarks gaily painted and chequered and hung with the shields of knights and with red pavises as a defence against archery, their sails embroidered with swans and antelopes, snakes and birds and all the creatures of heraldry, their ensigns and standards edged with feathers that rustled in the wind.

Until the arrival of the Archbishop of Bourges the King had been on the coast supervising the embarkation, and now that the French delegation had gone home again, he returned. He was a master of detail and he was a tireless worker. He rarely slept for more than five hours, often getting up before dawn, and he spent little time over his meals, eating whatever was put before him, without either pleasure or complaint. He left little to others that he could do himself and even corresponded himself with his master masons and carpenters and encouraged them to write to him from 'tyme to tyme of all matiers that seemed necessarie or expedient to signiffie'.

While engaged on this work at Porchester Castle in the third week of July, he discovered a plot 'most ominous as a presage for the future'.

It appeared that Richard, Earl of Cambridge, younger brother of the Duke of York, with the King's Treasurer, Lord Scrope, and Sir Thomas Grey, had conspired to assassinate the King and his brothers and replace Henry with another king over whom they could exercise control through the ramifications of their family relationships. The Lollard, Sir John Oldcastle, was to raise a new rebellion in the West; Henry Percy, Hotspur's son, was to raise the North; and there were to be risings in Scotland and Wales.

The Earl of March, son of the man recognised by Richard II as heir apparent, was one of the two men selected as the possible future king; but he was a timid conspirator, and the night before Henry was due to be murdered he revealed the whole plot to him.

The King acted with characteristic determination A commission headed by the Earl Marshal was immediately appointed and a jury of twelve Hampshire men empanelled. The three accused, Cambridge, Scrope and Grey, were all found guilty and Grey was summarily executed. The two others claimed trial by their peers and since there were so many in the district waiting to embark, this privilege could be accorded them without delay. Within a week they, too, had been condemned and executed. Henry had already returned to his army.

Family grievances had been at the root of the plot but it was assumed that the conspirators 'hadde receyved a huge summe of money, that is to say a million of gold, for to betraie the King and his bretheryn to the Frenschemen'. Like the tennis-ball story, it was probably not true, but it was, also like the tennis-ball story, good propaganda for war.

⚜

On 7 August 1415 Henry left Porchester Castle and in a small boat sailed down Portsmouth harbour to the coast. He had made all his personal arrangements for departure, and had bidden formal farewell to the Mayor and citizens of London:

44

'Heyle, comely Kyng', the Mair gan say
The Grace of God now be withe thee,
And speed thee well in they journay,
Almyghti God in Trinite,
And graunt thee evermore the degree,
To fell thin enemys bothe nyght and day.'
'Amen', seyde alle the comunalte.
'Grauntmercy, sires', our King gan saye.

He had said his prayers and made offerings at St Paul's and at St George in the Fields; he had said goodbye to his stepmother, Queen Joanna; and he had made his will, writing at the end of it, 'This is my last will, subscribed with my own hand, H.R. *Jesu Marcy and Gramercy. Lady Marie help!*'

On 10 August he went on board the *Trinité Royale* and gave orders for the mainsail to be hoisted to half mast as a signal for the other ships to close up.

It was a hot day of bright sunlight with a gentle breeze that lifted the unfurled forked banners of the knights and the square pennons of the bannerets from the masts. It took all day for the immense convoy to take up position and, as it did so, one ship caught fire and the flames from it spread to two others and all three of them had to be abandoned. It was a slight enough loss but coming so soon after the assassination plot it was considered a bad omen and the King was advised not to leave the country. Already the ships collected, despite their numbers, had proved insufficient to carry the thousands of troops and horses and the vast quantities of armour, weapons, equipment and supplies and much had had to be left behind. The burning of these three badly needed boats was surely a warning from God. The King, however, ignored these forebodings. He felt, as so many military leaders had felt and were to feel, that God was with him. There had been an unfortunate accident, nothing more. He would not turn back.

And so, at three o'clock on Sunday afternoon 11 August 1415, with drums beating on deck and trumpeters blowing their horns, with sailors shouting and priests praying, the great armada weighed anchor and sailed south.

⚜

The Earl of Dorset, the King's uncle (afterwards created Duke of Exeter), led the convoy as Admiral, with two lanterns at his masthead. The wind was strong out at sea and the painted sailcloth bulged tightly over the decks. In the clear sky above the *Trinité Royale* a flock of swans gathered. The burning of the boats was forgotten. The omens were good now.

The French expected the invasion at Boulogne—as the Germans were to do in 1944—and the Flemings were keeping watch from Nieuport to Sluys. Henry, however, had other plans, though few in the English fleet even now knew what they were.

'Concealing from all but his most intimate Council the direction in which they were to sail', one of his chaplains wrote later, 'he planned to cross to Normandy to recover first of all his own Duchy, which is his fully by right since the time of William I, the Conqueror, though now, as of long time past, it has been withheld from him against God and all justice by the violence of the French.' [A]

It meant nothing to Henry that King John had been disinherited of Normandy in 1204. The decision was wrong and illegal and he would reverse it. Afterwards, perhaps, he would turn south towards Gascony or inland towards the heart of the Kingdom of France; and, indeed, the contracts he had made with his officers had mentioned both of these places. To campaign in either south-western France or in the Seine valley, however, although he still possessed Bordeaux, would be a dangerous enterprise unless he had a firm foothold in Normandy, further south than Calais. The French would be fighting near their bases; he far from his, and his long lines of communication would stretch over an uncertain sea. But, if he could conquer an important port within striking distance of Paris, he would have gone a long way towards overcoming the disadvantages of his lines of supply and of fighting in a country where he possessed no strongholds and the enemy possessed so many.

There was such a port at the mouth of the Seine and his fleet had not been long at sea when he told his officers that they were sailing for it. It was called Harfleur.

⚜

The army's first glimpse of land was of the great chalk headland in the Seine estuary, three miles to the west of the town, known to

the French as the Chef de Caux and to the English sailors as Kid-
cocks, and during the afternoon of 13 August anchors were dropped
here.

On the northern shore of the estuary the troops on deck could
see the small port of Leure and the clustered buildings of the village
of St Denis, which has long since disappeared under the shingle and
shifting sand that would soon destroy the importance of Harfleur
itself and which would make necessary the building of the new port
of Le Havre further down the estuary to the west.

Harfleur in 1415, however, was still a busy and prosperous town,
one of the most important ports in France. There were thriving
trades of weaving and dyeing as well as fishing, ship-repairing and
smuggling. There were profits to be made from the salt marshes that
stretched, deserted and desolate, along the estuary shore, as well as
from the harbour; and inland beyond the wall of the town the land
was green and fertile. It was this wall, high and castellated, that
dominated the scene.

It stretched around the heart-shaped town for two-and-a-half-
miles and it was pierced by only three gates—the Montvilliers gate
in the north-east, the Leure gate at the south-west and the Rouen
gate at the south-east. Each gate was approached by means of a
drawbridge stretching across the moat which encircled the wall as a
protection against mining and each drawbridge was protected by
a portcullis. At intervals along the wall between these gates were
twenty-six towers, every one with a figure on top painted in blue
and gold—a lion, a dragon, a stork, a swan, a snail, a stag and other
figures less easily identified. Seen from the sea where the fleet were
at anchor by the Chef de Caux, it was impossible not to admire the
beauty of the town, its gently curving walls and towers and painted
emblems shining in the sun, and its background of wooded hills.
But to the experienced soldier's eye it was forbidding as well as
beautiful. Many lives would be lost in taking it.

⚜

By unfurling the royal banner at the masthead of the *Trinité Royale*
the King gave the signal for the summoning of his Council. It was a
large council for three dukes—York, the King's cousin, Clarence

and Gloucester, his brothers—eight earls, two bishops—Norwich and Bangor—and nineteen barons were with the expedition and felt as much right to be consulted because of their birth and large retinues as others had because of their experience. In fact, nearly the whole of the peerage—which then numbered only forty-one—was present. The Earl of Warwick as Captain of Calais, the Earl of Westmorland on the Scottish frontier and the Earl of Devon who was old, were the only three earls not there. But large and experienced as the Council was, Henry, by virtue of his strong personality as much as of his rank, was its evident master.

He did not hesitate to seek advice and often followed it—a circumstance which requires more emphasis than is usually accorded it, particularly by those who see in Henry V as in other young mediaeval kings astonishing qualities of born and natural generalship—but his character was at all times decisive, and there were occasions when he insisted on following a course of action he had already determined upon, against the opinion of the majority of the leading officers in his council.

In this, the first Council of the campaign, however, there was no discussion nor any need for it. The King's orders were brief and clear. No troops were to disembark before morning lest they should wander off in search of plunder; and before dawn a patrol, led by Sir John Holland, Sir Gilbert Umfraville and Sir John Cornwall, was to go ashore to reconnoitre. Darkness fell in silence.

The Siege of Harfleur

And to the town of Harflew there he tok the way
And mustred his meyne faire before the town,
And many other Lordys I dare well say,
With baners brighte and many penoun;
And there they pyght there tentys a down,
That there embroudyd with armys gay;
First, the Kynges tent with the Crown,
And all other Lordes in good aray.
    Wot ye right well that thus it was.
    Gloria tibi trinitas!

⚜

Once more unto the breach, dear friends, once more;
Or close the wall up with our English dead.
In peace there's nothing so becomes a man
As modest stillness and humility:
But when the blast of war blows in our ears,
Then imitate the action of the tiger;
Stiffen the sinews, summon up the blood,
Disguise fair nature with hard-favoured rage;
Then lend the eye a terrible aspect;
Let it pry through the portage of the head
Like the brass cannon: let the brow o'erwhelm it
As fearfully as doth a galled rock
O'erhand and jutty his confounded base,
Swill'd with the wild and wasteful ocean.

4

Between six and seven o'clock on 14 August 1415, 'the sun shining and the morning beautiful', the invasion of France began.

In hundreds of small boats the men were rowed towards the landing place, a long deserted beach of shingle and pebble drift strewn with rocks, three miles to the west of Harfleur where now stand the docks of Havre. Across the beach, deep ditches had been dug and banks of silt and pebbles had been thrown up to prevent the quick advance of an invading army. But these unmanned fortifications were the only sign that the English were unwelcome.

The troops jumped ashore and marched across the beach, filing in single columns round the dykes and through the narrow gaps in the banks, and then moved up in three columns over the salt marshes towards the wooded hills; and not a shot was aimed against them. A few peasants and fishermen could be seen scurrying away in the distance towards Harfleur, but there was no other sign of life.

Immediately on stepping from his boat, King Henry fell on his knees to pray that in the coming fight for his just inheritance he would have God's support. Then, having knighted several squires, he made for a hill about a mile to the north-west of the town and here pitched his main camp, ordering his brother, the Duke of Clarence, to take a detachment down into the farms and orchards between the hill and Harfleur, and the Earl of Suffolk to occupy a position with another small force on the inland slopes.

For three days, while the guns and siege equipment and the horses and stores were disembarked, the army remained in its position undisturbed, the King and his brothers spending their nights peacefully in the Priory of Graville.

On the day after the landing, the Feast of the Assumption of the Blessed Virgin Mary was celebrated with its normal pomp and solemnity and the King's priests performed 'their sacred services, at the usual hours, as if they were at home in a state of peace'. Already the pavilioners had erected all the royal tents; and heralds, minstrels, surgeons, chaplains and choristers, painters, carpenters and pages, grooms and clerks, officials of the buttery, the ewery, the napery and the spicery, of the poultry, the bakehouse and the kitchen, the wardrobe and the counting house, moved about busily between the gaily emblazoned marquees in the warm sunshine.

Below them, along the white lanes which led to the scattered farms and villages of the Seine valley, groups of marauders and foragers could be seen straggling off in search of food and plunder, prisoners and women. During the campaigns of Edward III in France, the English soldiers had earned the reputation of being 'very devils', far more to be feared than native bandits. And now as farmhouses burst into flames and churches were pillaged, it began to be feared that the English army would prove itself as merciless and avaricious as it had done half a century before.

What made the army so difficult to control when not in battle was its heterogeneity. Henry V's army was much more of a national force than the armies that had left England in the previous century; but it was far from being a native one. Apart from the foreign *condottieri*, as varied both in race and character as the indentured mercenaries they led, there were still numerous Irishmen and Gascons in its ranks as well as Welshmen and Englishmen. To exercise over it the sort of authority that could be exercised over a purely national militia was always extremely difficult and sometimes impossible. Henry, however, was determined to do everything he could to enforce the discipline without which no army can survive. Threatening plunderers and freebooters with the most severe punishments allowed by his military ordinances* was not, therefore, so much an act of charity towards the people whom he considered, in any case, to be his own subjects, as a necessary step towards forming an orderly army out of a hybrid array in constant danger of disruption.

The King, accordingly, lost no time in reminding his army of the fate that awaited the miscreants within its ranks. It was not only a

* A list of these ordinances believed to have been in force at the time is given in Appendix IV.

capital offence, he told them, for a soldier to kill a woman, it was not only a capital offence to rape her; even to enter a room where a pregnant woman was lying in such a way as to endanger her life or that of her baby rendered the culprit liable to lose 'all his goodes half unto him that accuseth him, and halfe unto the Constable and Marshall, and himself to be dede but if the King gave him his grace'.

Any man who entered a church to plunder it or who presumed 'to take any hallowed vessel, or ornament pertaining to the altar, books, or other things necessary for divine service' did so upon pain of death. And should he touch the Sacrament, he was to be drawn as well as hanged.

Neither the punishments nor most of the regulations were new, and, in issuing a proclamation which brought them to the attention of his soldiers, Henry was not extending the scope of English military law. Various additional ordinances which were promulgated during these first few days of the campaign were, however, ones to which his men had not previously been subject. They were now compelled, for instance, to wear—for purposes of recognition at all times and not only when fighting—a large red St George's cross on both chest and back. They were deprived of the company of harlots who were informed that they came within three miles of the camp at the risk of having their left arm broken after the first warning. And they were forbidden to take carts and oxen from the local inhabitants or to hold any child under fourteen to ransom.

While taking measures to bring his army under firm control, Henry was also concerning himself with tactical problems. So long as the disembarkation continued he could do little but make arrangements for the collection of provisions and the careful regulation of guards and outposts to prevent a raid by the French army which might by now have collected. But as soon as the landing was complete he could despatch part of his force to complete the investment of the town by establishing a blockade on its eastern side.

On 18 August he did so. That night the Duke of Clarence with a column of cavalry and infantry left his camp at the foot of the hill and moved out towards the far side of the town. The Duke was obliged to make a wide detour as the French had dammed the streams in the valley and flooded the roads that ran through it. This was not, however, altogether a disadvantage, for while splashing through a ford on the circuitous route that they had been obliged to follow, Clarence's troops came upon a column of wagons on its way to Harfleur from Rouen. After a short fight, all the wagons were captured and when the Duke of Clarence appeared on the high ground to the east of the town in the morning sunlight he was in possession of 'guns, vessels of powder, arrows and cross-bows in great abundance'.

Harfleur was now completely surrounded. The King stood to the north of the town, the Earl of Suffolk to the west, the Duke of Clarence to the east, and at the mouth of the Seine to the south was the English fleet. Henry called upon the garrison to surrender, telling them that all Normandy was his by right and that his town of Harfleur must be handed back to him. But the summons was indignantly refused by the garrison commander, the Sire d'Estouteville, who replied, '*Vous ne nous avez rien donné à garder, nous n'avons rien à vous rendre*'.

⚜

There seemed at this stage good reason for d'Estouteville's confidence. At the time of the English landing, his garrison had numbered less than a hundred men but on 18 August, three or four hours before the Duke of Clarence cut across the route to the east, the Sire de Gaucourt had entered the town to take command on orders from the French King and had brought with him 300 men-at-arms. The town's force was still a small one, but Harfleur's defences, already strong by nature, had been skilfully improved.

The three gates were protected not only by ditch, drawbridge, portcullis and flanking tower, but the approaches to them were all barred by earthworks, well-built barbicans and counter-approaches of earth and timber, each surrounded by a water-filled ditch. The barbican which protected the south-west gate, where an assault was most likely to be made—since the north-eastern gate faced out across the flooded valley and the south-eastern gate towards the river—was an immense round structure that reached 'nearly to the height of the walls of the town, fastened around, bound, and girded together very strongly' with fascines and tree trunks clamped together with iron bands. The garrison could enter it by means of

King Henry laying siege to a French town
From John Rouse, 'Life and Acts of Richard Beauchamp, Earl of Warwick,' c. 1485

a movable bridge across the moat and once inside could shoot at the besiegers through the slits in its face with both guns and cross-bows.

The river Lézarde flowed right through the town from north to south, but it entered the walls between the Montvilliers and Leure gates through tunnels guarded by a watergate, and where it left to flow out into the tidal waters of the Seine estuary a strong tower had been built on either bank. Iron chains stretched across the river between the towers and 'stakes and trunks of trees, thicker than a man's thigh', had been driven 'in great bodies' into its bed. At low tide the sharpened tops of these stakes stuck out threateningly above the water-line, and at high tide, when the water ran up into the town to fill the harbour, they disappeared below the surface while re-maining as great a hazard to enemy boats.

The defenders of Harfleur had, therefore, good grounds for believing that they could hold out until the French army came to relieve them, and by the end of the first week it seemed that their hopes might be realised.

⚜

The English had by then been forced to accept the facts that to starve the town into surrender would take far longer than they could afford and that an immediate assault was out of the question. Yet to break the walls before an assault presented problems almost as great. Battering rams could not be used because of the wide moat, while the accurate shooting of the garrison from their com-manding towers showed clearly how dangerous would be the opera-tion of drawing up the heavy guns as close to the walls of the town as they would have to be in order to damage them.

Henry had, therefore, decided to make his way forward with the spade. By digging trenches and tunnels he hoped to be able to get his miners in a position from which they could undermine the walls and open up a breach through which his men-at-arms could make their assault. But the French proved themselves quite as energetic miners as the English and far more skilful. They dug counter-paral-lels and sank counter-mines with such speed and accuracy that Henry was obliged to abandon this method of attack, and risk the dangers of pushing forward his guns.

The traditional method of protecting the carpenters and labourers, while the gun emplacements were being constructed, was to erect enormous screens made of closely bound planks fixed with hinges to stakes rammed firmly into the ground. When the gun was in position in its trench or on its wheeled platform, the screen could be pulled up for firing and then dropped again to protect the gunners from the enemy's counter-shots. At Harfleur these screens were used, but the commanding position occupied by the town's defenders made them more than usually ineffective and many English soldiers were killed before a single heavy gun was in position. Nor did the French rely solely upon what could be shot or thrown at their enemies from the safety of the town. Frequently groups of men-at-arms sallied out through the gates and charged across towards the English soldiers struggling with their ropes and levers in the fearful heat of the August sun; and after one such sally three English knights were dragged back to the town as prisoners.

Enterprising as de Gaucourt and d'Estouteville were, however, in conducting the garrison's resistance, their numbers were too few to prevent the guns from opening fire at last. And as they did so men marvelled at the noise they made.

Although clumsier versions of them had been in use for almost a hundred years, they were still a curiosity, these 'great gunnys' of cast iron that 'blew forth stones by the force of ignited powders'; and the biggest of them, twelve feet in length with a calibre of over two feet, were given nicknames—'London', 'the Messenger', 'The King's Daughter'—by the soldiers who watched them with proud amazement as they roared and rolled in the smoke. They hurled entire millstones at the town and soon the masonry of the towers and the earthwork in the bulwarks began to crumble, and great hunks of stone were knocked out of the walls and fell down into the streets of the town with a 'frightful noise'.

The gunners fired by night as well as by day and they poured tar and tow over the gun stones and set them alight before ramming them down the muzzle, so that they might set the timber-work of the barbicans on fire as well as break it up.

For more than a week the great guns roared at the town, hurling stones that weighed as much as 500 pounds at the walls; and when a gun broke down, as it often did, a more traditional part of the siege train was there to take its place. For despite the recent improvement of artillery, ancient methods of catapulting stones were still commonly employed. Arblasts, bricoles, mangonels, springalds, robinets and trepgets, and other machines with names as strange and mechanisms as improbable, were not to be abandoned for many years to come. They had a longer range than most guns, were more reliable and more manœuvrable, and some of them were almost as destructive. Indeed by 3 September they and the guns had done so much damage to Harfleur, particularly in the northern part of the town, that the King was sufficiently encouraged to prophesy confidently in a letter to Bordeaux—in which he asked for more guns and 600 casks of wine to be sent to him—that within another eight days the town would be in his possession and he would be on his way to Paris.

He had taken little rest since the landing. By day he laid new and careful plans, supervised administrative details, made reconnaissances, visited the gun emplacements and the outposts; by night he walked down from his camp to talk to the men on guard and give them hope and encouragement.

Many of them needed it. The days were still so hot that even to stand still in armour was exhausting, and to move about in it scarcely endurable; and at night the air that was borne by the breeze across the salt marshes was dangerously tainted. The heat, the unhealthy air, the inactivity of most of those who were not on duty with the guns and catapults, the flies that buzzed drearily around the open ordure pits and the horse pens, the prolific supplies of indigestible cockles and mussels that swarmed that year in the muddy creeks, and of unripe grapes and other fruits that the men could not be prevented from eating, and the gallons of new local wine that they could not be prevented from drinking, had already undermined the spirits and now threatened the health of the entire army. Cases of dysentery became more and more common; the Earl of Suffolk and the Earl of March contracted it, and the young Bishop Richard Courtenay of Norwich died of it after five days of suffering, and the King, who had loved him, sadly closed his eyes. Supplies of fresh beef, flour and good wine were sent to the sick from the royal stores, together with fresh eels and pike and sturgeon that fishermen from the Cinque Ports, on orders issued by the King before sailing, were catching for him along the Normandy coasts; but the sickness had got too strong a hold now, and scores of men were dying every day.

By the middle of the month Henry had good cause for sharing the army's deep depression. The optimism expressed in his letter to Bordeaux at the beginning of the month seemed no longer justified. There was dysentery, too, in Harfleur, but there is no reason to suppose that the King knew of it. And, indeed, the way in which the breaches made in the walls during the day's bombardment were regularly and thoroughly repaired each night and filled with bags of sand were evidence only of an unremittingly spirited resistance. 'I should not be altogether silent in praise of the enemy', wrote an Englishman who witnessed the siege. 'They could not in the judgment of man, have resisted our attacks with greater determination and skill.' [A] Also, the sallies out of the town by mounted men-at-arms continued without interruption, while repeated attacks were made upon the fleet in the estuary and upon the smaller vessels which sailed up and down the river, tenuously keeping communications open between the Duke of Clarence and the rest of the army beyond the flooded valley. Inside the town, the defenders returned the English fire as fiercely as ever with gun stones and flaming arrows wrapped round with tow dipped in resin; and they collected along the summit of the walls at every place where an assault seemed likely, buckets filled with lime and sulphur and hot oil and fat which could be tipped out on to the heads of the enemy through the machicolations.

On 16 September, when the main barbican outside the south-west gates—on which the English gunners had concentrated their fire for more than a week—was so badly damaged that its collapse into indefensible ruins was obviously imminent, the garrison acted with characteristic energy and resource. Rushing out of the gate behind it with sudden and unexpected force, a squadron of men-at-arms galloped across to the English lines, succeeded in reaching the trenches before the besiegers had recovered from their surprise and set an extensive part of their fortifications and two gun emplacements on fire.

This sally was, however, the last successful one that the French were able to make. Over a fortnight before, a messenger had been lowered over the walls of the town and had crept through the English lines to tell the Dauphin of Harfleur's perilous condition. But no help or encouragement had come. Both food and ammunition were running low, and dysentery was spreading fast. It was obvious that, unless a relieving force appeared very soon, Harfleur would fall to the English King.

Obstinately resolute to the last, however, the garrison made a final desperate sally from the town on 17 September, but this time it was little more than a brave gesture of defiance. The French troops were driven back in confusion and the young Sir John Holland, later, as a reward for his services, to be created Earl of Huntingdon (a title forfeited by his father for treason in Henry IV's time), counter-attacked with vigour, justifying the trust that Henry had placed in him. His men-at-arms rushed across towards the ruined and fiercely burning barbican, stumbled across the bundles of sticks with which they had filled up the moat, clambered over the remains of the palisade and forced their way inside. The French, distracted by the flames which they had unsuccessfully tried to extinguish during the assault, had offered little resistance to the charge, and were now compelled to fall back across the bridge which spanned the moat behind them, and to run for safety towards the open gates of the town.

The Fall of Harfleur

The engynes seide, 'to long we abyde,
Let us gon to ben on assent.'
Wherever that the ball gan glyde,
The houses of Harflew they all to rent.
An Englyssh man the bulwerk brent,
Women cryed, alas! that they were bore.
The Frensshmen said, 'Now be we shent,
From us this toun now it is lore.
  Wot ye right well that thus it was.
  Gloria tibi trinitas!

⚜

Open your gates. Come, uncle Exeter,
Go you and enter Harfleur; there remain,
And fortify it strongly 'gainst the French:
Use mercy to them all. For us, dear uncle,
The winter coming on, and sickness growing
Upon our soldiers, we will retire to Calais.
To-night in Harfleur we will be your guest;
To-morrow for the march are we addrest.

5

The loss of the barbican outside the Leure gate decided the outcome of the siege. So long as they held on to it, the leaders of the garrison were prepared, despite the spread of dysentery and the rapidly decreasing stocks of arrows, to continue their resistance until their food and ammunition were quite exhausted. But now that the English would be able to drag their heavy guns yet closer to the walls, they were persuaded that the time had come to negotiate. Already the towers had been 'rendered defenceless by the bastion falling in ruins; and very fine edifices, even to the middle of the city, either lay altogether in ruins, or threatened an inevitable fall, or were so shaken as to be exceedingly damaged'. [A] The terms that Henry offered the enemy, however, were so severe that the Sire de Gaucourt felt obliged to refuse them and to give notice that on no account would the keys of Harfleur be handed over so shamefully.

Henry accepted this answer without attempting to change de Gaucourt's mind by modifying his demands, and gave orders for an assault the next day. No effort was made to hide this decision from the French. Proclamations were openly and loudly 'made in the midst of the squadrons that all the sailors, as well as those soldiers who were on the stations assigned to them by their captains, must be prepared on the morrow to storm and mount the walls'. [A] At the same time all the guns, and all the other instruments of siege warfare, opened up on Harfleur in the fiercest bombardment to which the garrison and its inhabitants had yet been subjected. Stone balls and millstones crashed into the already battered walls, and flew over the walls into the dust-covered town behind. Many more houses were reduced to rubble and immense chunks of masonry were torn out of the steeple of the church of Saint-Martin and thrown down into the streets below where the wounded lay untended amongst the corpses.

For most of the night the bombardment continued, while in the light of torches the English finished their work on the ladders which the assault parties would use next day. Before dawn, however, messengers ran out of the town on the eastern side where the bombardment was less intense and went up to the Duke of Clarence's camp with a new offer to negotiate. The offer was accepted and the Earl of Dorset, Lord FitzHugh and Sir Thomas Erpingham, an old and faithful knight 'grown grey with age', were chosen to lead the English delegation. The French opened the discussion by asking for a truce until 6 October when, if no relief had come by then from outside, they would surrender. This suggestion was immediately rejected by the English who said that unless the garrison surrendered unconditionally the next morning the fight must go on. This apparently uncompromising attitude induced the French to make a more acceptable offer by agreeing to surrender the following Sunday, 22 September, at one o'clock in the afternoon if no relief had arrived. The new proposal was accepted, and the Sire de Hacqueville and twelve citizens of Harfleur were allowed to leave for Vernon to inform the Dauphin of the town's conditional surrender and to ask for help before the term of grace expired.

The agreement was signed; and twenty-four important men from Harfleur were handed over as hostages to the English army. 'Do not be afraid', Benedict Nichols, Bishop of Bangor and one of the King's chaplains, assured them, 'and do not suspect that we will do you any harm. Our lord, the King of England, does not come to France to ruin the country which by right is his own. He will not behave at Harfleur as your own countrymen behaved at Soissons. We are good Christians.' [c]

The following morning, as if to demonstrate the truth of his last assertion, Bishop Nichols, dressed in full pontificals, went up to the walls of the town, past the still smoking ruins of the bastion. Thirty-two chaplains, each in a surplice, amice and cope of bright silk and cloth of gold, and thirty-two esquires, each carrying a lighted torch, went before him and in his hands he carried the Eucharist on which both French and English swore that they would observe all the provisions of the truce agreement.

For three days the guns were silent. The weather continued stiflingly hot and the hours of inaction passed slowly. Dysentery spread in the English camps. Michael de la Pole, the Earl of Suffolk, died of it, and William Butler, Lord of the Manor of Warrington, and John Philip of Kidderminster and hundreds of others whose names have long since been forgotten. The Duke of Clarence contracted it and the Earls of March and Arundel, and by the end of the third week in September more than 2,000 men had died or were due to be sent home, and far more than this were ill.

Both sides anxiously awaited the return of de Hacqueville and his delegation from the Dauphin at Vernon.

⚜

The Dauphin, who had been appointed Captain General of all his father's military vassals, had reached Vernon on 3 September. But three weeks later he had done little to overcome the jealousies and antagonism of the rival factions that had been called upon to come to the defence of the country. In a sense, indeed, France was scarcely yet a country at all; and the common danger of invasion had brought about few reconciliations and but half-hearted attempts at unified resistance.

Charles VI had written from Paris a determined and dignified reply to Henry's letters:

> As none of your predecessors ever had any right, and you still less, to make the demands contained in certain of your letters presented to us by Chester your Herald, nor to cause us any trouble, it is our intention with the assistance of the Lord, in whom we have singular trust ... to resist you in a way which shall be to the honour and glory of us and of our Kingdom, and to the confusion, loss and dishonour of you and your party.

At the beginning of September he had taken the *Oriflamme*—the sacred red silk banner of St Denis which was the symbol of national resistance—from its guardians in the Cathedral of St Denis and had marched to Mantes. But his summons for service roused little more enthusiasm than his son had engendered further north at Vernon.

Charles d'Albret, Constable of France, was at Rouen attempting to assemble an army, while advocating the adoption of the Fabian tactics of Duguesclin, and Jean Boucicaut, Marshal of France, had a slowly growing force under his command at Honfleur, on the southern shore of the Seine estuary opposite Harfleur. Both of them, however, had already discovered that, while the Orleanists remained for the most part unco-operative and the Burgundians evasive, French people as a whole were more anxious to resist the suddenly oppressive demands of the tax collectors than the English troops. D'Albret and Boucicaut, both highly talented men, were also handicapped, of course, by the antiquated feudal structure of the French army in which pay was unthinkable, co-operation difficult to ensure, and effective discipline impossible to enforce.

The Duke of Burgundy promised to give his help but found repeated excuses for not doing so, refusing to let his only son Philip, Count of Charolais, join the army as he wanted to and keeping him locked up in the Castle of Aire near St-Omer where he burst into tears of frustration.

It was widely believed, in fact, that the Duke was only waiting for his rivals to move all their forces away from Paris before entering it in triumph himself; and others suggested that at any moment he would walk into the enemy's camp and come to an agreement with the English King that would destroy the power of the Orleanists. When an Orleanist was appointed Captain of Picardy, the Duke refused to recognise his authority, and most of the lords in the Burgundian dominions followed his example and refused to serve under the Dauphin without their overlord's permission. At the same time the Orleanists, of whom Charles was almost equally suspicious, answered his summons with evident reluctance; and although the Duke of Orléans himself sent 500 men, promising to follow in person later, both the Duke of Bourbon and the Duke of Berry withdrew their promised support in protest at what they claimed were the scandalous intrigues of the Dauphin.

And so it was that when the Sire de Hacqueville returned to Harfleur from Vernon he was able to bring with him no promises of help. The conditions of the truce agreement therefore had to be fulfilled. The town surrendered.

⚜

On Sunday afternoon, in a silk pavilion on the outskirts of his camp on the hill opposite Harfleur, Henry, looking 'as lordly as did ever any King', sat waiting on a throne draped with cloth of gold, for the keys of the town to be delivered to him. On his right was Sir Gilbert Umfraville, bearing on a pike-staff the King's tilting-helmet surmounted by his crown, and around him were gathered all his most noble knights in their 'richest apparel'.

Raoul de Gaucourt and Lionel de Bracquemont, accompanied by the twenty-four French hostages and several distinguished knights, walked up towards King Henry through a path formed by two ranks of English soldiers. A priest bearing the host walked before them and all of them, in submission to a humiliating order which the English King had imposed upon them, were wearing—as the burgesses of Calais had been obliged to wear in the presence of his great-grandfather, Edward III—'shirts of penitence' with ropes fastened round their necks.

The Sire de Gaucourt was met at the entrance to the English camp by a group of English lords who conducted him and his attendants to a marquee where they were obliged to kneel down submissively for a long time. They were then conducted to another tent and told to kneel down again. The humiliation was imposed upon them a third and even a fourth time in yet other tents, before they were permitted to enter into the King's presence.

But even now the King 'would not reward them with a look, until they had long knelt, and then he rewarded them with his look and gave a sign to the Earl of Dorset that he should take their keys from them. This the Earl did.'

Having impressed his victims with the power and authority of the English crown, Henry now displayed to them his condescension. Speaking to them for the first time, he reminded them that they had withheld his town of Harfleur from him 'in defiance of God and all justice'. Yet 'as they had given themselves up to his mercy, he would not be merciless'. [B]

He provided them with an elaborate supper and told them that they and all the people of Harfleur would be fairly treated.

The following day he announced his plans for their future in greater detail. Harfleur had already been an English town by right, he claimed; now he would make it an English town in fact, as Calais

THE FALL OF HARFLEUR

was. Merchants and tradesmen would be encouraged to come out from England and settle there by grants of houses and privileges for themselves and their heirs for ever, and proclamations would be made in London and other large towns to make this offer known. The present French inhabitants, all of whom were considered to have been taken prisoner with the garrison, would be allowed to remain in Harfleur provided they took an oath of allegiance to the English King. This concession was not, however, to apply to those who were old or poor or weak and who would consequently be out of place in a frontier stronghold; nor was it to apply to those who were rich enough to pay worthwhile ransoms for their freedom. If this ransom could not be paid immediately, the captive would be shipped over to England until it was paid.

As it happened, though, few citizens were taken on board the English fleet. Most of those who could afford to pay a ransom were allowed to retain their freedom for the moment on condition that they presented themselves at Calais on 10 November. De Gaucourt, sixty knights and 200 gentlemen were also released on parole for the same period so that they might have an opportunity of raising the money required. It was hoped, too—though this was not formally admitted—that the reports they gave of the conduct of the English King might win him support for his cause.

For this conduct, however it may appear to the modern mind, was considered mercifully just by his contemporaries. Even the expulsion of the town's poor and infirm was not condemned by them.

Two thousand of these pathetic victims of war, together with the women and children and priests of Harfleur, were sent out of the town the day after the English King entered it. He came in on Monday morning, dismounting at the gate over which his banner and the banner of St George were already flying, and went barefoot to the scarred chapel of Saint-Martin to spend two hours praying and offering thanks to God for his victory. The victims left on Tuesday, each carrying a small bundle and five sous which was all they were permitted to take with them, 'amidst much lamentations, wretchedness and tears'. They were provided with an escort as far as Lillebonne; but before they reached Saint-Aubin-de-Cretot they had been robbed of their money by French bandits and some of them had been stripped of their clothes.

Those who stayed behind in Harfleur were less unfortunate. Evidently the twenty-five-year-old Duke of Gloucester rode round the town threatening to hang all inhabitants who did not make a true declaration of their possessions, for the King had declared, as was customary, that all movables were forfeit to the victorious troops. But the plunder eventually taken was far less than had been expected; and its distribution was carefully controlled, each man being rewarded 'according to his rank and merit'; and only a few of the finest treasures being shipped aboard the *Trinité Royale* for the King's own use.

Within a short time the Earl of Dorset, the newly appointed Governor of Harfleur, and his lieutenant, Henry Verney, were able to report that the life of the town had returned to its former peaceable prosperity. The ships *Catherine* and *The Holy Ghost* arrived from Winchelsea loaded with provisions and stores including beer and oats, rope, glue and coal. Soon many English merchants and artisans had accepted the offers made to them of new homes and careers there, and English masons and tilemakers were at work repairing the damage caused during the days of siege.

⚜

Encouraging to Henry as the fall and occupation of Harfleur was, however, he could not but feel concerned about the prospect of carrying on with the subsequent operations upon which he had set his heart. Before Harfleur fell he had already had to recognise that his resources for an autumn campaign were extremely slender. In his letter to Bordeaux written on 3 September he had confidently envisaged a triumphant march along the banks of the Seine to Rouen and Paris and then 350 miles south-west to Bordeaux. Now it seemed unlikely that he would even be able to cover a quarter of that distance. Of the 9,000-odd men who had sailed out of the Solent on 11 August, many were now dead, most of them from disease which had seriously affected the vitality of thousands of others who had contracted it but who had survived. Many of these survivors were now too ill to take any further part in the campaign and had to be sent home to Southampton; and amongst these were many leaders including the King's brother, the Duke of Clarence, and the

Earls of Arundel and March. In addition to these invalids, the King would be obliged to leave more than a thousand men behind in Harfleur as a garrison, so that if he marched inland he could count on an army little more than half as strong as that which had sailed.

He was, though, despite his difficulties determined to march, provided a challenge to personal combat which he sent with Guienne Herald and the Sire de Gaucourt to the Dauphin on 26 September was not accepted.

This challenge* proposed that the English King and the French Dauphin should fight to decide who should succeed to the throne of Charles VI on the demented King's death. It asked the Dauphin to consider the dangers to Christendom of two great Christian nations fighting each other rather than joining together in alliance against the Infidel. 'For it is better for us, cousin', the King wrote, 'to decide this war for ever between our two persons than to suffer the unbelievers by means of our quarrels, to destroy Christianity, our Holy Mother the Church to remain in division, and the people of God to destroy one another.'

Neither the complacently pious tone of the challenge nor the fact that it was issued by a twenty-eight-year-old man to a sickly youth of nineteen was distasteful to the fifteenth-century mind. The personal combat was not so much a test of skill and strength and courage as a form of trial in which God would award victory to the just. The Dauphin's defeat would prove to the Christian world that Henry's cause was the cause of Christ. Henry himself never doubted that it was so, nor that he would win; but his victory would not be evidence of personal prowess, but proof of God's favour. Both his friends and his enemies saw the challenge in this light; and although neither can have expected the challenge to be accepted, Henry gave notice that he would wait eight days in Harfleur for the Dauphin's reply.

During these eight days Henry's ambitious plan for a march inland and a battle with any army that might presume to block his path, were discussed and criticised by his more cautious advisers. There were, indeed, many objections that could be raised to it. The military value of the *chevauchée*, which had become so custo-

* A translation of the challenge is printed in Appendix V.

mary a feature of warfare, is still, indeed, in doubt. French historians are generally inclined to support Sir Charles Oman's contention that this sort of pillaging expedition through enemy territory was not only heartless but aimless, providing no military excuse for the suffering it caused. Later English and American scholars, however, have seen the *chevauchée* as part of a long-term military plan designed to provoke the enemy into offering battle or at least to weaken his resources and powers of resistance if no battle were offered.

Whether or not considerations as to the military viability of *chevauchées* in general entered into the arguments propounded at Harfleur in October 1415, it is certain that many if not most of Henry's advisers found the particular *chevauchée* he now proposed unacceptable.

Because the expedition had been delayed so that the King could appear the injured party, unwilling to move before all attempts at a diplomatic solution had been frustrated, also because the Harfleur garrison had put up so spirited a resistance, September was already past and the season was getting very late for a campaign in foreign territory where an enemy army of unknown size was concentrating. This objection was particularly valid in view of the size of the English army which was known only too well.

The diminished strength of the Earl of Arundel's retinue provided an example of the fate of the component parts of the English forces. The Earl had left England with 100 men-at-arms and 300 archers. Now he himself was seriously ill and was waiting in the care of five attendants to be taken home to die; twelve of his men-at-arms and sixty-nine of his archers were waiting to be sent home with him; two of his men-at-arms and thirteen archers were already dead. Some retinues had suffered worse than Arundel's so that when all the dead were buried, all the ill shipped home, all the many deserters counted, and a garrison provided for Harfleur, the army would depart on its dangerous mission with about 6,000 more or less fit men—less than 1,000 men-at-arms and scarcely more than 5,000 archers. To march through Dieppe and Rouen to Paris with such a force would be an absurd undertaking. And God did not bestow victories on rash fools, however just their cause.

At a War Council held on 5 October, objections to the King's plans were put forward emphatically. Henry seems already to have abandoned by then his earlier project of a challenging march as far as Paris; but, supported by some of his younger and more ambitious officers, he argued with determination against the alternatives which were put forward—the establishment of an English enclave round Harfleur on the style of the Calais Pale or the evacuation of all the troops with the exception of those who formed the Harfleur garrison —and insisted that both honour and duty demanded an advance into his country which the French King was wrongfully withholding from him, if not, then, as far inland as Paris, at least as far north as Calais.

The risks involved in such an enterprise were, of course, enormous; but Henry was counting on the continued inaction and confusion of the enemy. They had left undisturbed his siege of Harfleur. Might he not reach Calais before their quarrels and mutual jealousies had been sufficiently overcome for them to collect an army strong enough to put in the field against him? And even if they did offer battle, might he not expect to defeat them by repeating the tactics of Crécy? He had reason to suppose that the Duke of Burgundy had professed loyalty to the French King, but he also had reason to hope that the Duke's support would be limited to protestations of sympathy and promises of future help. And the Duke's equivocation was, he believed, symptomatic of a national attitude.

The Dauphin was known to be at Vernon with a force of uncertain strength. But Calais is the same distance from Vernon as it is from Harfleur. A lightly equipped army, without guns—which would all be left in Harfleur or shipped to Calais—and with all its baggage and supplies on pack animals instead of in carts, could cover the 120 miles far more quickly than a recently assembled and more cumbrous force. Even if both armies began marching on the same day—the English for Calais, the French for a position where the route to Calais could be blocked—there would be little chance of the heavily burdened French outpacing the fast-moving English columns. Nor was it to be expected that the French would, in fact, start on the same day as the English, for it would not be known in the French camp (which was 100 miles from Harfleur) when and in what direction the English had gone until many hours after their march had begun.

Reports had by now come in of another French force under

Constable d'Albret collecting at Rouen which is a day's march nearer to Calais than Harfleur and Vernon. But Henry could reasonably suppose that this, too, would be unable to catch him once he had made his quick and unexpected start; and that even if it did manage to intercept him, it would not attack him unless supported by the force which the Dauphin had collected at Vernon. Marshal Boucicaut's force at Honfleur, it could also be supposed, would not attack until it had joined the rest of the army.

Henry's ability to reach Calais before the French forces could combine and block his path depended, of course, upon the quickest route being negotiable. There are ten rivers that flow into the Channel between Harfleur and Calais, and following the most direct route necessitates crossing them all. Of these only the Somme, however, is a serious obstacle and this, as his great-grandfather had discovered on his way to victory at Crécy, could be forded five miles downstream from Abbeville at Blanche-Taque where twelve men could cross marching abreast. It was essential, he knew, that this ford should be kept open for the passage of his army, but he had already taken measures to ensure that it would be, by instructing the commander of the garrison at Calais to send a force south towards the Somme in a diversionary movement which would attract any French troops there might be in the area away from Blanche-Taque. Sir William Bardolf, the Lieutenant of Calais, had, in fact, already sent 300 men down towards the Somme.

The Council listened to Henry's proposals with scepticism and anxiety. Many of them were older and more experienced men than he, and they felt sure that he was urging them on to disaster. The Earl of Arundel, claiming the insight of a dying man, said he felt confident that, if the King advanced inland from Harfleur, the Duke of Burgundy would hesitate no longer, but throw all his power into the scale against him; and others agreed with him, emphasising the dangers even if the Duke of Burgundy remained irresolutely neutral. They were all aware, though, that there were reasons other than purely military ones that were influencing the King's decision. The principal conspirators who had plotted to assassinate Henry and proclaim the Earl of March king in his place had been executed; but there were many others still alive who could hope to profit through the successful prosecution of a similar conspiracy. And the Earl of

March, who had been kept out of their reach by being brought out to France with the expedition, would soon be home and presumably well again. The ignominious return of Henry, without means to pay his creditors, after so confident and portentous a departure could not but lower his prestige—far yet from being unassailable—and would certainly create the sort of conditions in which a fresh plot might succeed. Further, to return now having gained but a single town at so high a cost, would make the raising of money and the winning of parliamentary support for a return to France to assert his right to her crown a far more difficult enterprise than it had recently proved. If, on the contrary, he were to march quickly yet flamboyantly from one English fortress to another through the lands he claimed as his own, even though the French denied him a victory in the field, he would have demonstrated his prowess and his right to return. In any event he was certain that God would not desert him.

'I am possessed with a burning desire to see my territories and the places which ought to be my inheritance', he told the Council in a final burst of enthusiastic piety and determination that silenced their doubts.

> Even if our enemies enlist the greatest armies, my trust is in God, and they shall not hurt my army nor myself. I will not allow them, puffed up with pride, to rejoice in misdeeds, nor unjustly, against God, to possess my goods. They would say that through fear I have fled away acknowledging the injustice of my cause. But I have a mind, my brave men, to encounter all dangers, rather than let them brand your King with word of ill-will. With the favour of God we will go unhurt and inviolate, and if they attempt to stop us, victorious and triumphant in all glory. [B]

It was the end of argument. Two days later carrying enough food for eight days—as the countryside was believed to be stripped of supplies—with no guns and few carts, Henry's small army marched out of Harfleur and set off north along the road to Calais.

The March Across the Somme

Our Kyng rood forth, blessed he be,
He sparid neither dale ne doun,
By townes grete, and castell hyghe,
Tile he com to the water of Som.
The brigge the Frensshmen hadde drawe a doun,
That over the water he myght nought ryde.
Our Kyng made hym redy bown,
And to the water of Turwyn he com that tyde.
    Wot ye right well that thus it was.
    Gloria tibi trinitas!

⚜

We would have all such offenders so cut off; and we give express charge, that in our marches through the country, there be nothing compelled from the villages, nothing taken but paid for, none of the French upbraided or abused in disdainful language; for when lenity and cruelty play for a kingdom, the gentler gamester is the soonest winner.

6

The English army left Harfleur, in its by now traditional formation of three main bodies with flanking detachments, between 6 and 8 October and marched north towards Montvilliers. Sir Gilbert Umfraville and Sir John Cornwall commanded the vanguard; the King, with his brother the Duke of Gloucester, Lord de Roos and John Holland, was with the main body; while the rearguard was led by the Duke of York and the Earl of Oxford. The troops carried little but their provisions and their weapons. The heavy armour of the men-at-arms was strapped to the backs of the pack animals who trailed along at the rear in the care of the knights' attendants. The few carts were packed with the sort of things without which a Christian king could not happily travel—the royal beds, the King's crown and seals, his silver spoons, his sword of state, the altar ornaments of his chaplains, his piece of the True Cross that a Welsh Crusader had brought back from the Holy Places.

Once again, as on landing, proclamations were made reminding the troops of the punishments which would be inflicted upon those who were found guilty of breaches of military law, and commanders were enjoined to impress upon their retinues the discipline and restraint which the King insistently demanded. They were told that the French were subjects of the English King and that they were consequently not to be ill-treated in any way nor to be plundered except for food in case of necessity. The persons of priests as well as of women and children were to be considered inviolate; churches were sacrosanct upon pain of death; even swearing was forbidden. Depredations were committed, of course, and one French chronicler asserts that at Fécamp, thirty miles north of Harfleur, the English troops set fire to the town, and those inhabitants who had not run

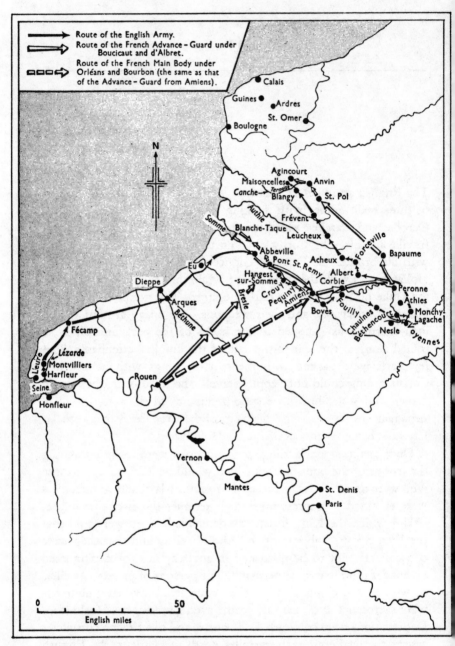

The March to Agincourt

away into the open country 'took refuge with their property in the abbey. The English sacrilegiously made a stable of the great altar, and of all the chapels; opened the coffers of the inhabitants, and carried off their effects; dragged the women from the church and ravished them.' [c]

But, although the English certainly did not behave as well as their own chroniclers suggest, accusations of wholesale brutality and uncontrolled looting were more properly applied to the armies of Edward III than to those far more strictly governed troops of Henry V. It may be true, indeed, as one of the French chroniclers suggested, that in the Agincourt campaign it was the French troops, neither more nor less violent and avaricious than the English but far less sternly disciplined by their leaders, who were guilty of the worst offences.

On 11 October the army reached Arques, four miles south of Dieppe. Running through the little stone-walled town was the first of the rivers that had to be crossed—the Béthune. It was narrow, though, and the bridge was undamaged and the troops moved down towards it having no cause to believe that they might not get across unmolested. High above the river, however, stood the château of Arques and suddenly from its towering walls a cannon opened fire.

There had been some slight opposition, already, at both Mont-villiers and Fécamp, but so slight had it been that the rearguard had scarcely had to slow its pace. But now the whole army was brought to a halt while the King prepared a message for the Castellan of Arques. The message took the form of the stern threat traditionally adopted in the face of such presumption offered to English armies on foreign soil. Addressing the Castellan as though he were an impertinent rebel rather than a patriot, the King commanded him to let his army pass over the bridge and told him that, if he did not do so, the town of Arques would be burned to the ground. The Castellan, convinced of the determination behind the threat, immediately gave way and, as if rendered excessively nervous by his previous display of spirited opposition, provided the English troops with a large supply of bread and wine to hasten them on their journey.

The following day the army marched a further twenty miles north and before nightfall had reached the river Bresle about half a mile to the east of Eu. Here again the leading troops were halted by a cannonade and later attacked by a strong force of French cavalry which came charging towards them through the gates of the town. The English held their ground and after a fierce fight, in which both sides suffered losses, the French men-at-arms were driven back into Eu. Henry now made use of the threat that had gained him the passage of the river Béthune the day before; and on this occasion, too, it was accepted as real. The river Bresle was crossed, bread and wine were once more brought into the English camp, and the troops settled down to rest in the farms and villages beyond the grey stone walls of Eu.

Since leaving Harfleur the army had now covered eighty miles and had suffered little loss. Two rivers had been crossed, and the next—the Somme—was only thirteen miles distant and by the ford near its mouth a cheerful meeting was expected with the force that had been sent out from Calais to keep the crossing open. Henry could feel content that so far things were going well. Some men were still suffering from dysentery but not as many as his more anxious advisers had feared, and as yet no one was hungry. A few stragglers had been captured but there had been no more desertions. In the morning he would set off again and by midday he would have reached the Somme at the Blanche-Taque ford.

Soon after dawn on 13 October the army turned out of its night quarters and started off again along the rough roads of Upper Normandy. Seven miles were covered without sight of the enemy and the men moved down hopefully into the valley of the Somme. About six miles from the river, however, the advance guard came across a solitary Frenchman and took him prisoner. The information he gave to the commander of the advance guard brought the whole army to a sudden halt.

The prisoner was taken back to the King, who was still marching with the main body, and he repeated his story to him. He was a Gascon, he said, and a servant of Constable d'Albret. The English could not hope to cross the Somme at Blanche-Taque, since the ford, into which strong and sharp stakes had been driven, was guarded by a force of no less than 6,000 men under Marshal Boucicaut.

This disastrous news was scarcely credible. When last reported the

1 *King Henry V*
From a contemporary painting by an anonymous artist

2 *Arming for battle*
From the 'Poems of Christine de Pisan', c. 1415

3 *Knights in combat*
From a late fourteenth-century misericord

4 *The English army at sea*
From a late fifteenth-century illumination

5 *English soldiers disembarking*
From 'Life and Acts of Richard
Beauchamp, Earl of Warwick',
by John Rouse, c. 1485

6 *Thomas Plantagenet,*
Duke of Clarence

7 *Michael de la Pole,*
Earl of Suffolk

8 *Bishop Beaufort of Winchester,*
the Lord Chancellor

9 *Sir John Holland,*
later Earl of Huntingdon

SOME ENGLISH LEADERS
From effigies on their respective tombs

10   *The end of a siege: English soldiers take a French town*
From a late fifteenth-century illumination

11 *Humphrey Plantagenet,*
Duke of Gloucester
From a contemporary drawing

12 *Sir Thomas Erpingham*
From the statue above the Erpingham Gate,
c. 1420, at Norwich Cathedral

13   *Soldiers on the march*

14   *Soldiers looting*
Both from illuminations of c. 1398

15 *Marshal Boucicaut*
From a contemporary illumination

16 *John, Duke of Burgundy*
From a painting of 1419

17 *French soldiers in a skirmish*
From an illumination of c. 1398

18 *English and French knights in a mêlée*
From an early fifteenth-century illumination

19 (*Overleaf*) *The Battle of Agincourt*
From an illumination in the St Alban's Chronicle, c. 1450

20 'La bataille dazincourt'
From an illumination in 'Les Vigiles de Charles VII', 1484

21 English and French calvary fight it out
From an illumination in the mid-fifteenth-century 'Chroniques de Normandie'

22 *Charles, Duke of Orléans, imprisoned in the Tower of London*
From a late fifteenth-century copy of 'The poems of Charles of Orléans'

23-4 *Henry's helmet and sword*
From his funeral achievements

25 *The King, with a sword*
From a mid-fifteenth-century watercolour

26 *Henry V on horseback*
From the counterseal of the Gold Seal
of Henry V, 1415

27 *Henry at the siege of Caen, 1417*
From 'Life and Acts of Richard Beauchamp, Earl of Warwick',
by John Rouse, c. 1485

28 *The marriage of Henry V and Catherine of Valois, daughter of Charles VI
From 'Life and Acts of Richard Beauchamp, Earl of Warwick',
John Rouse, c. 1485*

Marshal had been at Honfleur, nearly 100 miles away to the south. The King told the Gascon to repeat his unlikely story and that if he did not tell the truth this time he would have his head cut off. The man insisted that what he said was true; and the King called a council of war. While awaiting the return of scouts sent forward to verify the prisoner's story—there is no certain evidence that any scouts were sent, but it is inconceivable that they were not—the knights in council discussed the three possible courses that faced them. They could attempt to force the passage of the ford; they could, although already more than half-way to Calais, turn back to Harfleur; or they could turn inland and march east up the Somme valley in the hope that they might find another crossing place. The discussion lasted for two hours and while they talked the tide began to flow and the waters rose at Blanche-Taque, and no attempt could be made to force the ford until it ebbed again. And yet to turn back was unthinkable. The army turned east.

And as they marched up the river valley no longer sure of their route—for if their leader had a map it must have been a very simple one—their spirits, so the chroniclers say, began to falter and fall.

> I who write [recorded one of them] and many others raised our bitterly anxious eyes to heaven imploring for the mercy of the Almighty's celestial regard. And we besought the glorious Virgin Mary and the blessed St George, under whose protection the most invincible crown of England had flourished of old, to mediate for us between God and our poor people. [A]

⚜

On the northern bank of the river the enemy watched and followed them. The French army was now a large and formidable force. The fall of Harfleur seemed to have awakened a sense of national urgency. The Dukes of Orléans, Alençon and Bar had all at last answered their summonses and had joined the army with their retinues; and the Dukes of Bourbon and Berry had reconsidered their decision to withdraw their support. The Duke of Brittany, who had at first refused to serve, had also now arrived bringing 12,000 men. The Comte de Richemont had brought 500 lancers. The Duke of

Brabant and Count de Nevers had promised to join the army as soon as they could. Even from the dominions of the Duke of Burgundy many knights had now come, despite their overlord's continued equivocations.

At a council held at Rouen, although Charles d'Albret and Marshal Boucicaut were known to favour purely Fabian tactics which would exhaust the English army, combined with an attempt to regain Harfleur, it was decided by a vote of thirty to five to 'pursue and fight the enemy'.

All over the country threatened towns were fortified and garrisoned and stores collected. Men practised their archery by day and at night kept watch with dogs and lanterns outside the moats. Peasants and tradespeople, as well as men-at-arms and archers, came to the royal standard, and, though treated contemptuously by many knights who wondered what the army wanted with a lot of useless shopkeepers, the citizens of Paris offered 6,000 well-armed men 'to fight in the front on the day of battle'.

The rejection of these Parisians was, indeed, in a sense justified for the French forces now numbered about 60,000 men, including about 15,000 men-at-arms. Admittedly 20,000 were ill-armed peasants and artisans from Picardy, Artois, Normandy and Champagne; and about half the total number, excluding cross-bowmen, were valets, pages, grooms and attendants, and '*gens sans aveu "bandits, bâtards" qui suivaient les armées pour l'espoir du pillage*', like birds of prey drawn by the smell of corpses. But the total number of fighting men was already far in excess of the number that the English could bring into the field.

It is not known for certain, and cannot now be discovered, when and by what route the vanguard of these forces left their quarters on the Seine and marched to the far side of the Blanche-Taque ford. But it seems likely that Boucicaut had moved east from Honfleur and joined Constable d'Albret at Rouen by the time the Dauphin received the English King's challenge, and that both Boucicaut and d'Albret had moved quickly north to the Somme with an advanceguard to destroy the crossings round Abbeville as soon as it was learned that the English had left Harfleur. Certainly by 12 October Boucicaut and d'Albret had overtaken the English and were on the north bank of the river, preparing to drive the invading army upstream towards the main French forces which would soon be converging on Péronne.

❧

The day after they had turned up river from the strongly defended ford at Blanche-Taque, the English troops approached Abbeville. Here, on the following day, 15 October, they hoped to be able to cross over to the northern bank. But once more they were disappointed. Scouts reported that the bridge at Abbeville had been made impassable and there were large numbers of French troops on the far side. So the columns moved on again, marching south-east for Pont Rémy; and, finding that no crossing was possible there either, they moved on again towards Hangest-sur-Somme. For the whole of the following day and for most of the next they marched upstream, moving further and further away from Calais in their search for a crossing place, passing through Crouy and Picquigny eight miles north-west of Amiens.

Food was getting short now. Many men had finished their rations and were living on nuts and dried meat—mostly nuts for they were 'shrewdly out of beef'. They had nothing to drink but water, as wine was reserved for the knights.

Spirits were sinking ever lower. The nights were colder but the days almost as warm. The houses and farms by the wayside were barred and silent and the countryside had been stripped of all that might fall into the hands of the oncoming foreigners. Occasionally a group of French scouts was seen watching them from the far bank, but it was otherwise as if Picardy had been deserted by a people driven out by famine.

Whenever the army halted a group of men would dash off towards a farmhouse and, finding it deserted and the fields around it stripped of food, they would set it on fire so that if the track of the army was momentarily lost, René de Belleval said, '*on l'eût bientôt retrouvée à la fumée des incendies qu'il allumait sur ses pas*'.

On 16 October the leading troops reached the village of Boves and here, as at Arques and Eu, shots were fired at them from the castle, and as before the King agreed to spare the buildings and crops on condition that his troops were allowed to continue their march undisturbed. They did not pass on immediately, however, for in the village they had found 'an abundance of wine in open casks' and were drinking it up as fast as they could. Numbers of men were already drunk and many others were crowding round the casks filling their water-bottles, before the King learned of it. Immediately he discovered what was happening, however, he gave orders that no more wine should be drunk; and when someone suggested that the men might at least be permitted to fill their water-bottles, he turned on him angrily. Bottles, indeed! He did not mind bottles. But most of them had already 'made bottles of their bellies', and had got very drunk. [D]

The men obeyed the order with surly resignation. Each step they had taken for the past four days was a step further away from Calais, further away from home, and no nearer it seemed to the French army. The countryside was lifeless and empty and when they did see something worth taking, which was very rarely, they were forbidden this traditional indulgence of an army on the march. Now they were not even allowed to drink wine, and yet the knights and esquires had it.

Aware of the grumbling discontent amongst the archers the King reacted in a characteristically firm and decisive manner. On the day after the army left Boves, a man was discovered to have stolen a pyx with the host in it from a church and hidden it in his sleeve. He was led bound through the ranks so that all should see him and all should know the punishment soon to be inflicted upon him. He was hanged on a tree and the army was made to march by his body silently.

At Corbie, eight miles north-east of Boves, the archers had something else to grumble about. For here a large force of French knights galloped suddenly across the bridge and knocked down several Englishmen before any resistance could be offered to them. Eventually they were driven back; and several prisoners were taken and some of these prisoners said that the French knights were determined to get to grips with the English archers. They intended to charge them at full tilt and to ride them down while they were still fumbling to get their arrows out of their belts or pulling back their bowstrings.

The King resolved to prevent this by a simple expedient. On the

Duke of York's suggestion, he ordered each bowman to cut himself a stout stake six feet long and to taper both ends to sharp points. At the sight of French horsemen the stakes were to be rammed into the ground at an oblique angle pointing towards the enemy, so that there would be formed a sort of *chevaux de frise* on to which cavalry would ride at their peril and behind which bowmen could shoot in relative safety. It was an ingenious device, and the archers were eventually to be grateful for it; but for the moment they were more conscious of the fact that they had an extra burden to carry and an unknown distance to carry it. They knew they could not hope to be at Calais for at least another week and perhaps much longer, for it had become generally accepted that the French army, now rumoured to number 100,000 men, would contest every remaining crossing place between Corbie and the river's source, still a dispiriting number of miles away to the east.

But at Fouilly near Corbie, the King—perhaps on information received from the prisoners he had just captured—decided to change the direction of the march. Instead of following the course of the Somme eastwards to Péronne and then south along the wide curve of the river, he turned southwards immediately and made for Chaulnes and Nesle across the chalk downland. Such a move had an obvious advantage: the French on the north bank of the Somme would have to cover the two sides of the triangle formed by Corbie, Péronne and Nesle, while the English were marching along the third side at the base. It might then be possible to reach Nesle, where the river was fordable, before the main body of d'Albret's forces could get there, and before the outposts guarding this lower crossing could reasonably expect the English to arrive at it.

On the morning of 18 October the army left its quarters southeast of Fouilly and after marching about twenty miles came close to Nesle where the next night was to be spent. The men were tired and hungry and ill-tempered as they pushed their way into the farms and cottages north-east of Nesle, and the peasants, whose unwelcome guests they were, watched them with sullen hostility. Some of these peasants had hung out of their windows cloths and flags, coloured red like the *Oriflamme*, as a token of defiance; and the King, angered as always by this display of independent spirit by a people whom he considered his subjects, gave orders that their homes and crops would be burned to the ground the next morning unless they demonstrated a change of attitude by practical help.

During the night, under pressure of this threat, some peasants came to the royal tents and asked to see the King. Anxious to see the last of the English army, they told him that there were two fords at Béthencourt and Voyennes a few miles to the north-west. Scouts sent out to reconnoitre these fords came back to report that they were unguarded. The opportunity to get across the Somme at last could not be missed and orders were given for the army to turn out before dawn and to be ready to march at a moment's notice.

In the darkness of the early morning of 19 October, the troops moved out of their billets. The men-at-arms and archers marched on the road to Voyennes, the pack animals and carts on the road to Béthencourt. Both roads led across marshy ground that soon became a swamp. Across this swamp through which a little stream, the Ingon, made its sluggish way into the Somme, the roads were built up on causeways, and only by keeping to these narrow causeways could the river be reached. But about half a mile from the river, the leading troops discovered that the final length of the causeway had been broken up.

The army could not turn back now, though, and then continue their search for an alternative crossing place still further upstream, for the advantages of the march across the downlands from Fouilly would then be lost. And so, by some means, Henry was determined, his men must get across here.

The first necessity was to send forward a detachment of lightly-armed bowmen with instructions to clamber across the broken causeway to Voyennes as best they could, to wade through the ford, and then to form a bridgehead on the high ground beyond the far bank, driving off any French troops they might find there. Soon 200 archers, their bows slung across their backs, were making their way from foothold to foothold across the treacherous swamp. They managed to reach the river at Voyennes and to splash into the ford. The water came almost up to their waists but the bed beneath their feet was firm, and before midday they had all reached the far side.

Meanwhile, behind them, Henry had given orders for the broken causeway to be repaired and men were already cutting down trees in the woods, pulling down all the buildings in the neighbourhood and filling up the rough gaps so that the army could move quickly across. Trunks of trees, roof timbers, bundles of thatch, logs, doors, gates and the remains of crumbled walls were carried on to the causeways and wedged in the holes that the French had made in them.

The work had begun soon after eight o'clock and about four hours later the causeway which led to Voyennes was capable of carrying marching men; and the one further north which led to Béthencourt could carry animals and even, it was hoped, carts. The repairs were clumsy and ramshackle, of course, and in parts the men would have to pass over in single file; but now that the archers had succeeded in establishing a bridgehead on the other side, Henry could hope that his whole army might succeed in getting across before nightfall.

At one o'clock in the afternoon, led by 500 men-at-arms of the advance guard under Sir Gilbert Umfraville and Sir John Cornwall, the army began to move down to the river bank. The King himself stood at the head of one causeway where the fighting men were to cross to ensure that there was no confusion and to encourage his troops as they passed; while two of his knights performed the same duties at the head of the other.

Soon after the crossing began a force of French horsemen delivered an attack on the thinly held bridgehead but the archers, supported now by Umfraville and Cornwall and a few men-at-arms who had so far got across with them, succeeded in driving them off. And for the rest of the afternoon the crossing continued undisturbed. When the light began to fail it was almost completed and an hour after sunset the last man stepped out of the ford and on to the far bank.

The army was across the Somme; and although Calais was still well over 100 miles away, there were now no other rivers as difficult as this to cross.

The men went to sleep that night in their billets around Athies and Monchy-Lagache in far better spirits than they had enjoyed for several days.

As they slept, however, only six miles away to the north, the French army entered Péronne.

⚜

Marshal Boucicaut and Constable d'Albret, who had crossed the Somme somewhere near Abbeville on 12 October and had been shadowing the English ever since, had now joined up with the main body of the French army under the command of the Dukes of Orléans and Bourbon.

The King and the Dauphin had both wanted to lead the main body but they had been dissuaded by the old Duke of Berry who had fought at Poitiers where Charles VI's grandfather had been captured. It was bad enough losing a battle, Berry advised, without running the risk of losing the King too. The King accepted the advice of his old uncle and, appointing d'Albret Commander-in-Chief, he let Bourbon and Orléans go on without either himself or his son.

The two dukes had left Rouen on 14 October and had marched for Amiens, hoping, perhaps, to prevent the English—forced by Boucicaut and d'Albret to march up-river from Blanche-Taque—from advancing any further. The English, in fact, had passed Amiens when the French main body reached it on 17 October but now, two days later, it had got across their path at Péronne. And here, while d'Albret fell back to Bapaume to deepen the French position, still protesting that they should confine themselves to purely defensive operations, Orléans and Bourbon sent three heralds with a formal challenge to the English King, to tell him that they hoped they would meet him before he reached Calais and to ask him to name a suitable place at which to fight.

❧

When the three heralds arrived in the English camp they found the men resting. The evening before, the English troops had marched up from Voyennes and Béthencourt after their exhausting crossing of the Somme and today, Sunday 20 October, while the King awaited the return of scouts he had sent off at dawn in search of the enemy, they were allowed to have a few hours in which to sit and talk, to sleep, or dry their clothes or to try to find something to eat.

The heralds were taken to the Duke of York who took them to the King before whom they fell on their knees and remained silent until told to deliver their message.

'Right puissant Prince, great and noble is thy Kingly power, as is reported among our lords', one of them politely began when given permission to do so.

'They have heard that thou intendest with thy forces to conquer the towns, castles and cities of the realm of France and to depopulate French cities. And because of this, and for the sake of their country and their oaths, many of our lords are assembled to defend their rights; and they inform thee by us that before thou comest to Calais they will meet thee to fight with thee, and to be revenged of thy conduct.'

To which Henry, with a courageous spirit, a firm look, without anger, and without his face changing colour, calmly replied, 'Be all things according to the will of God'.

When the heralds asked what road he would take, he answered, 'Straight to Calais, and if our enemies try to disturb us in our journey, it will not be without the utmost peril. We do not intend to seek them out, but neither shall we in fear of them move either more slowly or more quickly than we wish to do. We advise them again not to interrupt our journey, nor to seek what would be its consequence: a great shedding of Christian blood.'

The heralds, satisfied with this answer, and being dismissed after receiving each a hundred gold French crowns, returned to their lords. [B]

Believing that his reply to their challenge would induce the French to attack him the next day, Henry addressed his men 'with great spirit and tenderness', and gave orders for them to occupy a defensive position facing Péronne where he now knew the enemy to be. All day long they looked for signs indicative of an impending attack, but the ground that sloped away in front of them towards Péronne remained quiet and deserted.

By the late afternoon it was clear that no attack was being mounted, and the men were told that they could spend the night in peace before setting off towards Calais in the morning.

Henry had not named a place for the battle that he could scarcely now avoid but he hoped that when the time came he would be able to find a position as favourable as the one he had discovered at Péronne.

⚜

On Monday morning, 21 October, the English march was resumed in heavy rain. The troops moved down into the valley of the little river Cologne and marched under the walls of Péronne. A few

French horsemen rode out of the town as though, an observer thought, they hoped to draw the marching columns within range of its walls; but on the English 'horsemen making a stand they quickly fled back into the town'.

Péronne was left behind and the army moved on towards Albert. Still there was no sign of the main body of the enemy who must, it now seemed clear, have abandoned their position in favour of another one further back. But then, about a mile outside Péronne where the road to Albert crosses the road to Bapaume, the English troops came upon evidence of an 'unimaginable host'. The wet surface of the road that led north-east to Bapaume had been freshly churned up by the feet of thousands of men on the march; and there could no longer be any doubt about the nearness of the enemy or the route he had taken.

As Bapaume was several miles to the right of the direct route to Calais which the English were taking, Henry believed that the enemy might be intending to attack him from this flank on the march, and, so that he might be warned of any such attack, he sent off an additional flank-guard to his right. Nothing of the enemy was seen, however; and for all that day the march to the north-west was undisturbed.

The heavy rain, blown into their faces by a strong wind, once more lowered the spirits of the tired and hungry men. The sight of the Péronne–Bapaume road, which they had crossed over that morning, had alarmed many of them. It had been, as one of them remembered, so 'strangely trodden' by so 'many thousands of the French army' that they could not but now dread the impending battle. The chaplains 'raised their hearts and eyes to heaven', as they had done when they had found the Blanche-Taque ford closed against them, 'crying with voices of the deepest earnestness, for God to have compassion upon us, and, of his infinite goodness to turn away from us the power of the French'. [A]

They marched sixteen miles that day on the road to Albert, with the flank-guards on their right making for Miraumont, and by the evening of the next day they had reached Forceville and Acheux. On October 23 they marched a further eighteen miles, passing the Count of St-Pol's castle at Leucheux without opposition and pressing north on the road to Frévent where there was a bridge across the

Canche river. Towards evening the King and his entourage lost
their way for a time as the advance-guard seem to have done on
previous days, and he passed by the village which had been selected
for his night quarters by the harbingers. But when he was told that
he had missed it, he refused to turn back. He, like all his knights,
had been wearing their *côtes d'armes* since the crossing of the Somme
and in this warlike costume he refused to retrace his steps. 'God
would not be pleased if I should turn back now', he said, 'for I am
wearing my *côte d'armes*.' [D] And so he went on as far as Frévent,
turning out the advance-guard which was already established here
and sending it on to the village of Blangy on the river Ternoise.

On 24 October, as Henry himself approached Blangy, the guards
on his right flank reported that 'many thousands of the enemy',
whose line of march had been more or less parallel with his own
since Bapaume, were now drawing closer in towards him. He
quickened his pace but held to his route, following the advance-
guard across the narrow causeway which spanned the Ternoise
valley at Blangy and advancing towards the crest of the ridge which
rose 300 feet above the river.

A scout sent forward by the Duke of York had already reached
the summit of the ridge and had seen with a shock of dismay that
the French, who had crossed the Ternoise at Anvin some time before
the English had crossed at Blangy, were now streaming across the
valley to the right in three immense columns, 'filling a very wide
field, as with an innumerable host of locusts'. [A]

They were marching, as the scout could clearly see, slowly towards the lines of the English advance with their countless arblasts,
ribaudequins, baggage carts and guns, and would soon be astride it.

The scout 'retreated with a trembling heart and with the utmost
speed his horse would carry him to the Duke of York, and being
almost breathless, said, "Quickly, be prepared for battle, as you are
just about to fight against a world of innumerable people".' [A]

The Duke turned his horse and galloped down the slope to the
King who received the news calmly, 'neither changing into a cold
tremor, nor into the heat of passion, but, having ordered the main
body which he directed in person to halt, he hastened at the utmost
speed of the fine horse on which he rode, to view the enemy'. [E]

They were still pouring past him beyond the valley to his right;

but although he now knew he could not select his own position for battle, he remained calm, 'committing himself and his army to God's protection', and riding back to seek the advice of his most experienced soldiers.

Soon the English army was deployed in line, with all horsemen dismounted, along the top of the ridge facing the enemy. As the French, too, began to deploy, the King's priests went through the ranks hurriedly hearing the confessions of the many men who clamoured for absolution. The King also passed along the ranks 'animating the men with his intrepid demeanour and consoling expressions' and when one understandably apprehensive knight, Sir Walter Hungerford, regretted in his presence that they did not have 10,000 more English archers, the King turned upon him scornfully and rebuked him with a characteristic speech:

'Thou speakest foolishly, for by the God of Heaven, on whose grace I have relied, and in whom I have a firm hope of victory, I would not, even if I could, increase my number by one. For those whom I have are the people of God, whom He thinks me worthy to have at this time. Dost thou not believe that the Almighty, with these His humble few, is able to conquer the haughty opposition of the French?' [A]

As it happened, however, there was no call for the humble few to perform the work of God that day, for the French commanders, realising the folly of offering battle to the English army while it occupied so commanding a position, and realising too, perhaps—as at least one chronicler thought—that it would soon be dark and chivalrous leaders did not carry on war at night 'as it is not fit', wheeled their long lines into columns again. [A] And these columns, looking 'like so many forests covering the whole of the country far and wide', [E] then moved forward once more with inexorable and disconcerting ponderousness until they had pushed behind the woods of Tramecourt and sprawled right across the road to Calais.

Watching this operation, which finally blocked his march to the sea, Henry knew that the battle he had provoked could not now be avoided.

He moved his men down into the village of Maisoncelles. It was the eve of the Feasts of Saints Crispin and Crispinian.

Before the Battle

The Kyng knelyd doun in that stounde,
And Englysshmen on every syde,
And thries there kyssed the grounde,
And on there feet gon glyde.
'Christ,' seyde the Kyng, 'as y am thi Knyght,
This day me save for Ingelond sake,
And lat never that good Reme for me be fright
Ne me on lyve this day be take.
    Wot ye right well that thus it was.
    Gloria tibi trinitas!

⚜

'Tis not the balm, the sceptre and the ball,
The sword, the mace, the crown imperial,
The intertissued robe of gold and pearl,
The farced title running 'fore the king,
The throne he sits on, nor the tide of pomp
That beats upon the high shore of this world,
No, not all these, thrice-gorgeous ceremony,
Not all these, laid in bed majestical,
Can sleep so soundly as the wretched slave,
Who with a body fill'd and vacant mind
Gets him to rest, cramm'd with distressful bread;

7

It rained through most of the night. There was little shelter in the village and many of the archers lay down to rest beneath the thin cover of trees, in ditches and in the open fields. They were desperately tired and hungry. Many of them, and all the men-at-arms, had ridden the 260 miles from Harfleur, but there were those who had marched all the way with only one day's rest in seventeen; and for eight days now they had been carrying the heavy stakes they had cut in the woods near Albert and Miraumont, as well as their other weapons and between forty and fifty arrows stuck in their belts. Their clothes were torn and now wet through again; their shoulders sore. Some still suffered from dysentery or 'colde diseases', others had never fully recovered from earlier attacks. Most of them had eaten little but hazel nuts and bits of hastily roasted meat for the past three days. They had seen the vast size of the French army, and could scarcely hope for victory. Those who had not already confessed now did so and the priests knew that most of them expected soon to die.

The camp was very quiet. Earlier on, as the men milled about looking for food and drink and somewhere to sleep, as the armourers shouted to each other above the sound of their hammers and files, there had been so much noise that the King had threatened every knight who did not observe his rule of silence with the loss of a horse and harness and every 'inferior person' with the loss of his right ear. But so quiet, indeed, had the camp now become that the French outposts believed that the English had run away and that the few camp fires which could be seen flickering through the rain marked the boundaries of an abandoned position.

There was no doubt in the English camp, though, that the French were still there. Although they were half a mile away and although the sounds of their voices were muffled by the damp air, they could be heard shouting orders and calling out the names of servants and attendants long into the night. They had been standing to arms all afternoon; but as soon as word had gone round that there would be no battle that evening, the sudden roar and confusion reminded one chronicler of a country fair. Varlets ran off to find straw to strew on the muddy ground so that their masters could sleep in some sort of comfort; trunks and chests were unpacked; banners and pennons furled; nearby houses were pillaged and then burned '*pour le plaisir de destruire*'; great fires were lit near the numerous banners of the *commandeurs*; the baggage in the carts was pulled about by men in search of stores that might make the night less uncomfortable.

The noise and bustle were matched by the confidence. The English were known to be few and weak and tired and ill, incapable of resisting so strong a host of Frenchmen. They themselves had come a long way, of course, and had travelled as fast as their enemies; but they had fed well enough and what they had not been given by the country people they had had no compunction in taking; also very few of them had had to come on foot. They felt fresh enough to sit up talking and gambling with dice for the prisoners they were going to take—the worthless archers being valued at a blank—and they even felt confident enough, so it was said afterwards, to paint a cart in which the captured Henry V was to be paraded through the streets of Paris.

The English King, for all his apparent self-assurance and evident trust in God, could not fail to believe that the Frenchmen's loud jauntiness was justified. It was his usual habit to walk round his camp at night to see for himself that the orders he had given were being carried out, to talk to his soldiers and to impress upon them his own faith in their courage and spirit and in God's benignity. There is no record of his having done so this night, as Shakespeare suggests, but not to have done so would have been to break an invariable habit, and not to have recognised his soldiers' distress, and in it his own danger, to have been without feeling or thought.

Already he had felt obliged to offer the French terms so as to avoid fighting a battle at so great a disadvantage. Negotiators had gone over to inform the enemy commander that the English King was prepared to treat for an uninterrupted passage to Calais on the

Men-at-arms of 1415
From church brasses at Barsham, Suffolk, and Covenham, Wiltshire

basis of a renunciation of his right to Harfleur. The French had replied that he must not only restore Harfleur but renounce the title he pretended to the crown of France, being allowed to retain only what he held in Guienne. On receiving this answer Henry had slightly modified his original offer but, soon after nightfall, the unpromising negotiations had been broken off, with Henry's request that the now inevitable battle should be fought the following morning. The prisoners taken during the campaign were released on condition that they returned to him if God granted him the victory.

The night wore on; the rain continued to fall; the bowmen who could not sleep notched the shafts of their arrows and waxed their strings; the priests went round in the darkness hearing confession after confession; and men knelt on the wet earth 'with their clasped hands raised towards Heaven, praying that God would take them into his protection'. [D]

⚜

Before dawn on 25 October 1415 both armies roused themselves and began slowly to adopt the positions in which they were soon to fight. During the night Henry had sent some of his knights forward to survey the field of battle and had already decided how best to make use of its advantages.

The ground did favour him. Chivalry dictated, of course, that the chosen battle-field should offer opportunities for a fair and honourable fight; but the constricted position adopted by the French seems to have been taken up less from a desire to provide a battle-ground free from unfair advantages to either side as from lack of foresight. Hemmed in on their left by the Tramecourt woods, round which they had marched the day before, and on their right by the woods that surrounded the village and castle of Agincourt, this position, as can be seen from the plan, denied their army any of the freedom of movement that was essential to the successful deployment of so large a number of men.

It was already clear that the craft of Duguesclin and the lessons of Crécy and Poitiers had been forgotten or rejected. D'Albret and Boucicaut were both aware of the dangers in fighting the English in the style of a dead age; but they could not hope to bring their influence to bear on so vast, disorganised, quarrelsome and disparate an army. They could but prepare themselves to fight bravely in a manner that had altered little for at least three centuries, to stand their ground and hack about them until dead, worn out or victorious.

But even to hack about with axe or sword in those dense ranks would be an operation of unusual difficulty. And any advance that might be made during the course of the battle would narrow the front still further; for, although the two woods were about three-quarters of a mile apart where the French took up their first position, they were scarcely more than half a mile apart where the clash between the two armies might be expected to occur. Every step that the French took forward would, therefore, render them even less capable of mobility than they were already.

Henry had no such problem, for he had so far fewer men. Exactly how many fewer has never been established and cannot now be known. Contemporary estimates varied enormously, one chronicler suggesting that the French outnumbered the English by thirty to one, another by three to one. The only point of agreement between nearly all of them is that the disparity was very great and on this point—despite the recent attempts of the distinguished French historian Ferdinand Lot to prove them wrong—they were almost certainly right. The number of the French, in fact, as Lieutenant-Colonel Alfred H. Burne has convincingly demonstrated, must have been between 20,000 and 30,000, while the English forces—and there has been no argument on this point—numbered between 5,500 and 5,900 men. There can be little doubt, then, that the English were outnumbered by at least four to one, the proportion suggested, also, by Sir James Ramsay.

Henry drew up his men in a field of young corn between the southern ends of the woods about three-quarters of a mile from the French. Each army could see the other quite clearly, for the rain had stopped now and the field that stretched between them was almost flat.

The English formation—according to reports admittedly meagre and conflicting—consisted of three main bodies of dismounted men-at-arms, standing four deep, with wedge-shaped groups of archers on either side of them. On each wing there were, as shown in the

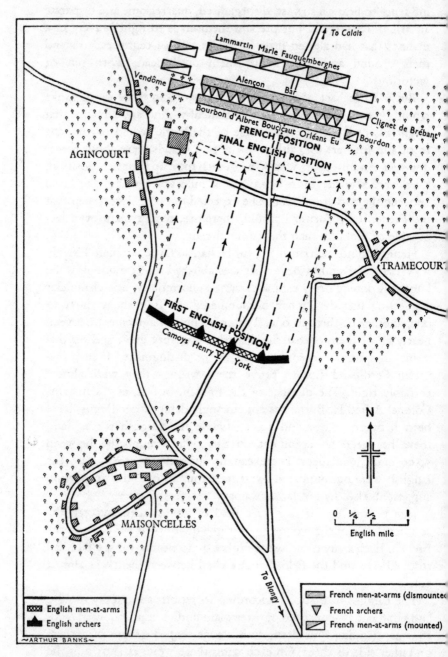

To Calais

Lammartin Marle Fauquemberghes

Vendôme

Alençon   Bar

Bourbon d'Albret Boucicaut Orléans Eu
FRENCH POSITION

Clignet de Brébant

Bourdon

AGINCOURT

FINAL ENGLISH POSITION

TRAMECOURT

FIRST ENGLISH POSITION

Camoys Henry V York

N

MAISONCELLES

0   ¼   ½   1
English mile

To Blangy

English men-at-arms
English archers

French men-at-arms (dismounted)
French archers
French men-at-arms (mounted)

~ARTHUR BANKS~

Positions of the armies between Agincourt and Tramecourt, 25 October 1415
(The position of roads and buildings and the extent of woods are all, of course, conjectural)

plan, a line of archers with their outward flanks curving in towards
the centre, so that the French, when provoked into attack, could be
subjected to a hail of arrows not only from the front but from the
sides as well. The Duke of York was placed in command of the men
on the right—the men who had formed the advance-guard during
the march—and Lord Camoys was placed on the left with those who
had been in the rearguard. The King decided to remain in the centre.

The French line was slightly longer and a good deal deeper. It
consisted almost entirely of men-at-arms who are spoken of as being
in three lines about five or six deep. The first two lines were dismounted, and there were a few archers and cross-bowmen between
them. The third line and the wings on either flank, where the guns
were also laid, were composed of men-at-arms who remained on
horseback. The arrangement sounds simple and neat and on the
plan, of course, it appears so. But it was, in fact, nothing of the sort.
For the pushing and jostling of knights to get into the first line and
into the first row of the first line was uncontrollable. 'All the lords
wished to be in the first battalion', a French chronicler recorded.
'For each was so jealous of the others that they could not in any
other way be reconciled.' [c] So congested, indeed, did the front
ranks become that the few archers seem to have been squeezed out
on to the flanks where the harassed gunners were trying unsuccessfully to keep open a satisfactory field of fire. In the end not only the
Constable d'Albret and Marshal Boucicaut managed to place themselves in the front line, but the young Duke of Orléans (who with
several others had recently been knighted), the Duke of Bourbon,
the Counts of Eu and Richemont and so many hundreds of other
knights that there seemed to one observer to be more banners
fluttering from lances in this line than there were lances in the entire
English army.

The English, however, now that the waiting was almost over,
appear to have been far less concerned about the inequality in numbers than they had been the night before. This, indeed, owed much
to the King whose powers of inspiration and leadership had never
been more advantageously displayed. He rode along the lines without spurs on a little grey horse followed by several pages leading
his other horses, one of which was a '*magnifique destrier blanc comme
la neige*'. He was wearing a suit of splendidly shining armour and a

surcoat embroidered quarterly with the arms of England and France, the leopards and the *fleurs-de-lys*. He spoke to the men, encouraging them and joining in their prayers.

Already he had called up the baggage from Maisoncelles, where it had been plundered by French marauders, and with it had come the sick, the pages, the sumpters, and the priests. The priests were commanded to come to the front of the army and to pray continually and not to return to the baggage until the fighting began. 'Remember us, O Lord!' they chanted. 'Our enemies are gathered together and boast in their might. Scatter their strength and disperse them, that they may know that there is none other that fighteth for us but only thou, our God.' [A]

'Amen', said the King. 'Amen', responded the troops, deriving strength from their faith in God and in the King who believed they were all fighting in His name.

With bare head the King knelt down to receive the Sacrament and, when he had said his last prayers and the third Mass he heard was over, he rose to his feet and put on his helmet. It was plated with pure gold and encircled by a gold crown studded with sapphires and rubies and 128 pearls.

Now dressed for battle and with his sword in his hand, he addressed the army in a loud clear voice,

> saying that he was come into France to recover his lawful inheritance, and that he had good and just cause to claim it, and in that quarrel they might freely and surely fight; that they should remember they were born in the Kingdom of England where their fathers and mothers, wives and children now dwelt and therefore they ought to strive to return there with great glory and fame; that the Kings of England, his predecessors, had gained many noble victories over the French; and that on that day every man present should do his utmost to preserve his own honour and the honour of the Crown of England. He reminded them that the French had boasted they would cut off three fingers from the right hand of every archer they might capture in order that they might never presume again to shoot at man or horse.

He told them, too, that he would rather be killed than taken prisoner as he would never charge England with the payment of his ransom. And when he had finished his soldiers called out loudly in reply, 'Sir, we pray God give you a good life, and the victory over your enemies'. [D]

✤

For four hours both armies held their ground, looking across at each other over the long cornfield in the dull morning light. The English archers, angered by the rumour which the King is quoted as having repeated, that the French would cut off their fingers, and angered too by reports that the French knights would spare no one who could not be sold for a good ransom, grew restless and impatient.

The French, on the contrary, despite their earlier frantic jostling for position, seem now to have been almost relaxed. In the crammed ranks of the first line some of the men-at-arms were sitting down on piles of muddy straw around their banners, eating and drinking, talking cheerfully, calling out to rivals to 'beg forgiveness' for their behaviour in some recent quarrel. Others who had spent the night in the saddle so as to keep themselves clean for the fight, remained standing for fear their armour would get muddy before the battle began.

In the less congested ranks of the second line, commanded by the Dukes of Bar and Alençon, there was more room for the knights to move about, and the clumsy and deliberate way in which they did so showed how heavy this armour was. Thick breast and back plates of steel reached as far as the knees; leg armour, bolted and jointed, met the steel boots at the ankle; heavy chain aventails, fixed to their helmets and in many cases covered with steel plate, increased the weight on their necks and shoulders. The helmet and cuirass of one knight—Ferry de Lorraine—soon to be one of the dead, alone weighed ninety pounds.

Even raising a hand encased in gloves of boiled leather, with steel backs and steel gauntlets, and an arm encased in steel sleeves, with steel joints at the elbow and shoulder and thick rings of chain mail under the armpit, was a movement requiring some strength in itself; but walking about with the full weight of armour on the back, the helmet on the head, weapons hanging from the belt and in the hand, and doing so on sodden ground so much churned up by horses that in places the mud was ankle deep, was an exertion that few men could make without soon becoming exhausted and none could make with grace. The prospect of fighting so encased and on such ground does not, however, appear to have caused these men-at-arms undue anxiety. Most of them had broken off the ends of their lance shafts, as to wield these long weapons in such tightly packed ranks was clearly going to be impossible, but this was the only concession made to the exigencies of the moment. They waited under their banners and behind the *Oriflamme,* which was borne by Guillaume Martel in front of the first line, and all the chroniclers agree that they waited with cheerful confidence.

There had been a great deal of argument earlier on as to whether they should attack or wait in this position for the English to attack them. The younger and more headstrong of the knights were for an immediate charge so as to settle the matter once and for all. The more experienced, including apparently both d'Albret and Bouci-caut, advised a prolonged wait, for then either the English must attack them and begin the battle at a disadvantage, or starve. This defensive policy had, in fact, been advocated by d'Albret and Boucicaut from the beginning of the campaign, since, as they insis-ted, by this policy Henry could be forced to surrender without a fight. They had been overruled on former occasions. But now they appeared for the moment to have convinced their more impetuous countrymen; and the argument had temporarily been settled. The French army appeared content to leave the initiative to the English.

⚜

As the morning wore on, Henry's confidence, real or assumed, began to waver. He had hoped that the French would have attacked him soon after dawn and would have exhausted themselves in doing so; but now, three hours after daybreak, they still remained motion-less. And he must fight his battle that day, for his men would be incapable of fighting it tomorrow. 'The army', as one of his chap-lains put it, 'was very much wearied with hunger, diseases, and marching, and was not likely to obtain any food in this country. The longer they remained there, so much the more would they be sub-jected to the effects of debility and exhaustion.' [A]

Henry sought the advice of the more experienced soldiers among his knights and asked them whether or not they thought he should attack as the enemy showed no signs of attacking him. They all agreed that he should, and he appeared to be ready to accept their guidance when three horsemen were seen to move out of the ranks of the French army and ride across towards him.

One of these horsemen, the Sire de Heilly (who had been taken prisoner by the English in a previous campaign and had escaped) went up to Henry and, without the polite preamble that custom and etiquette demanded, told him that he had heard it said that his captors accused him of having escaped 'in a way unbecoming a knight', and that if anyone dared to repeat the accusation he would challenge him to single combat and prove him a liar.

The King replied that there could be no question of personal quarrels being settled at such a time and advised Heilly to return to his companions and tell them to begin their attack.

'I trust in God', Henry added coldly, 'that if you did disgrace the honour of knighthood in the manner of your escape you will today either be killed or recaptured.'

Heilly refused to deliver the King's message. His companions, he said, were not his servants but subjects of the King of France and they would begin the battle at their own pleasure, not at the will of their enemy.

'Depart, then, to your host', Henry said dismissively, turning his horse's head. 'And however fast you ride, you may find that we shall be there before you.' [B]

It was nearly eleven o'clock. So far as could be seen from the English position, the French ranks were still motionless. They could not, Henry felt sure, be waiting for reinforcements. Perhaps, though, they hoped that the sight of their massive formations would oblige the English to surrender on their terms; perhaps they were hoping that illness and lack of provisions would have the same effect. In any event, they had lit fires again as though prepared to wait all day. But Henry determined that he himself could wait no longer.

He told Sir Thomas Erpingham, that faithful knight who had been his father's Chamberlain, to ensure that the archers were in their right positions and ready to shoot. Sir Thomas went over to marshal them, drawing them more closely into those arrowhead-shaped wedges in which they had been trained to stand while shooting, calling out words of encouragement to them as he did so.

They were dirty and ragged as well as hungry and tired. Their loose jackets were torn and wet and mudstained. Many of them were barefoot and some of them, according to one account based on uncertain authority, were naked, without even the hat of boiled leather, which had been their one protection against the swords of the knights, and wearing only the belt in which their arrows and clubs were stuck.

When they were all arranged to Sir Thomas's satisfaction, he threw his stick into the air and cried out 'Nestrocque!', the word (interpreted as either 'Now Strike!' or 'Knee! Stretch!') used by the Marshal of an army after finishing his duty of arranging it for battle.

Sir Thomas was answered by a loud shout from the archers; then he dismounted and his page led his horse to the rear. He placed himself near the King who was also now on foot at the head of his men with his banner borne before him.

A few minutes later Henry gave the command, 'Banners Advance! In the name of Jesus, Mary and St George!'

Immediately, as always before a battle, each man fell to his knees to make the traditional observance which symbolised the Christian warrior's recognition that in God's time he would return to dust and that, although he was desirous of it, he was unworthy to receive the Sacrament. He made the sign of the cross on the ground with his hand and then placed his lips on the earth and kissed it, taking a piece of soil into his mouth.

This silent ceremony performed, the men stood up and all three divisions moved forward. They marched slowly, steadily and firmly, 'in very fine order', shouting 'St George!' repeatedly, 'and with their trumpets sounding'. [D]

The Battle

They triumpyd up full meryly,
The grete bataille togyder yede.
Oure archiers shotte full hertyly,
And made Frensshmen faste to blede.
There arwes wente full good sped,
Oure enemyes therwith doun gon falle,
Thorugh brestplate, habirion, and bassonet yede.
Slayne there were xj thousand on a rowe alle.
    Wot ye right well that thus it was.
    Gloria tibi trinitas!

⚜

I was not angry since I came to France
Until this instant. Take a trumpet, herald;
Ride thou unto the horsemen on yon hill:
If they will fight with us, bid them come down,
Or void the field; they do offend our sight:
If they'll do neither, we will come to them,
And make them skirr away, as swift as stones
Enforced from the old Assyrian slings:
Besides, we'll cut the throats of those we have
And not a man of them that we shall take
Shall taste our mercy. Go and tell them so.

8

The English army went forward up the field and crossed the track
that led from Tramecourt to Agincourt. The earth was soggy under-
foot but unlike the ground over which the French were soon to
advance had not been so badly churned up by thousands of horses,
and the going across the untrodden furrows was not too difficult.
When they were within 300 yards of the French, and so just within
bowshot range, they halted and the archers thrust their stakes into
the ground making a series of sharp-pointed fences outside the front
ranks. Then each man returned to his place, took down arrows from
his belt, slid the notch into position along the greased string, pulled
back the shaft till the goose feathers were against his cheek and took
aim. There was a sound as of water rushing over a weir, and
suddenly the 'air was darkened by an intolerable number of piercing
arrows flying across the sky to pour upon the enemy like a cloud
laden with rain'. [E]

Thus provoked, the great mass of the French army lumbered into
life. The mounted men-at-arms on the flanks, or as many of them as
could push their horses through to the front, charged across the
cloggy mud at the archers on either side of the English line. They
galloped forward bravely, keeping their heads down so that the
arrows, which came flying towards them in a continuous stream, did
not hit them in the exposed part of the face, and they rode straight
at the fences of stakes. But only a few of them succeeded in getting
so far, and, having done so, the horses were immediately impaled
upon the sharp points and threw their heavily armoured riders at
the feet of the archers who soon clubbed them to death.

The rest of the horses were so infuriated by the arrow-heads that
tore deep gashes in their flesh that they became unmanageable and
either rolled on the ground in agony or ran away in all directions,

most of them straight back into the dense ranks of the dismounted men-at-arms now struggling forward under Charles d'Albret who had called upon them to confess their sins and to fight bravely.

Several knights were knocked down by the maddened horses and found it extremely difficult, even with the help of their pages, to get up again out of the wet and clogging earth weighed down as they were by their mighty cuirasses and heavy leg-pieces. The exultant shouts of '*Montjoie! Saint-Denis!*' that had filled the air at the beginning of the advance became desultory and angry. Like the horsemen, these dismounted men-at-arms had to keep their heads down to avoid the arrows which, even so, pierced through the sides and lower face-guards of many helmets.

So as to present what they hoped would be a less exposed target to the bowmen, the dismounted men-at-arms broke up the line in which they had started to advance and gradually formed themselves into columns. But the English archers directed their shots at the sides of the columns and managed to hit as many men as before; and this was the easier for the bowmen—particularly those on the edges of the English line—to do, since the French, already committed by the narrowing space between the woods, were slowly drawing in ever closer towards the centre of the line where their real and worthy opponents, the English men-at-arms, awaited their onslaught.

Struggling manfully and purposefully down the field, their ranks frequently broken by horses charging into them and tormented by archers whose shots from the flanks inclined those in the outer columns instinctively to push in towards the already conglomerated mass of the centre column, but yet refusing to accept the socially inferior archer as a seemly opponent for a knight in armour, the French men-at-arms approached the English line with traditional pride and bravery.

The few guns that earlier on had perfunctorily fired an occasional stone ball at the English line were now silent; and those few cross-bowmen who had not been squeezed out of their shooting position by the men-at-arms, fiddling with their crankins and clinches, their gaffles and their winders, were no match for the far quicker and far more accurate English and Welsh long-bowmen. So the men-at-arms came on practically unsupported.

As the distance between them and the English line narrowed, the pace of their advance quickened. It had become a commonplace of tactics that the knight when advancing must bear down upon the enemy at the greatest speed his armour permitted, so that the first shock of contact would throw the opposing line off balance. And the ground that the French were now covering permitted this traditional increase in speed for, although sodden, it had not been kicked up by horses into that liquid mud through which they had lately come. When the clash came, then, the force of their advance sent the men in the middle of the English line reeling backwards.

It was the first advantage that the French had so far gained in the battle. And it was to be the only one. For it soon appeared that the men-at-arms were so densely packed in their congested ranks that they had left themselves no room in which to fight. Indeed, many of them were squashed so tightly against their neighbours that they could not even raise their arms to strike a blow; and when others pushed on urgently from behind, several of them lost their balance and fell over at their opponents' feet. They could not get up, for there were no pages to help them, and in a moment they had either been hacked to death or crushed beneath the weight of other falling men and eventually suffocated.

So it was that in a few minutes the English line had rallied and were knocking over and cutting down Frenchmen in their hundreds. And the English archers 'perceiving this disorder of the French advanced-guard, quitted their stakes, threw their bows and arrows on the ground and seizing their swords, axes and other weapons, sallied out upon them'. [D]

Many dropped their own weapons as they ran and picked up the heavier swords and lances, hatchets and halberds, bill-hooks and maces, that the French had dropped in their confusion. Dirty, ragged and wildly excited, they threw themselves upon the men-at-arms and swinging their arms above their heads brought the heavy blades and leaden spikes down with fearful force upon the armour of the men-at-arms. Some were knocked down instantly, and the archers hacked at their faces and the weak joints in their armour; others managed to maintain their balance but were unable to ward off the well-directed blows of the nimble-footed bowmen, who, jumping about in their bare feet and loose shirts, found no difficulty in avoiding the slow parrying strokes of their enemies. Many other men-at-arms fell to the ground, stunned, slightly wounded or not hurt at all, and were held down there by the weight of others who tumbled on top of them. Hundreds died in this way, of suffocation. More, in fact, 'were dead through press than our men could have slain'. [F]

Soon the dead, wounded and suffocating were lying in heaps, two or three deep, and the archers clambered over the top of them to lash out at the men-at-arms still on their feet in the ranks further back.

The English men-at-arms, several of whom had been knighted that morning, were fighting furiously, too, and when the second French line, scarcely distinguishable now from the remnants of the first, came up with them, the slaughter continued unabated. For the closer the French pressed in to the centre of the fighting the less they were able either to swing their arms back to strike a blow or to raise their arms forward to parry one. Many of them, of course, when the fall of their companions gave them room in which to move, fought with magnificent courage.

The Duke of Alençon was one of these. Swinging his sword arm valiantly he held his own against the English knights and, having cleared a space around him, he mounted a nearby horse and galloped off in an attempt to rally the many men-at-arms who, dismayed by the fate of the advance-guard, were making away from the fight. He did not succeed, however, and rode back to the battle alone.

The story is related that he dismounted close to where the young and impetuous Duke of Gloucester was fighting and rejoined the battle there. Several other knights now rallied round him and they advanced towards Gloucester and his retinue. The English Duke was wounded in the stomach by a dagger which was thrust up beneath his breast plate and he fell to the ground. His eldest brother, the King, was fighting nearby, surrounded by guards, and as soon as Henry was told of his fall, he moved over to help him. When the King and his guards had pushed their way through to him, they found him lying down with his feet towards the enemy. They managed to drag him away; and in the ensuing fight the Duke of Alençon was knocked to the ground. Unable to rise, he lifted up his hand and called out to King Henry above the din, 'I am the Duke of Alençon, and I yield myself to you'. [G] Henry held out his hand to him, but as he did so, some Englishman, uncontrollably excited, smashed his battle-axe into Alençon's body and killed him instantly.

The King remained unhurt. He had fought so bravely already that day that men said afterwards that even had he been of the most inferior rank he would have earned himself greater renown than anyone else in the battle. He was helped by his guards, of course, and he was helped, according to one French chronicler, by there being two men dressed as he was and wearing crowns to mislead any knights who might covet the honour of killing him. But the chronicler who records the presence of these decoys—and the story is uncorroborated—mentions, too, that they were both killed. And certainly the King exposed himself constantly to a similar fate. The stories told of his unflinching valour were later embellished, no doubt; but his personal bravery at Agincourt is not a romantic conceit but a historical fact which is incontestable.

A body of eighteen knights, it is believed, led by Brunelet de Masinguehen and Ganiot de Bournonville, swore that they would get near enough to him to strike the crown from his head, or die in the attempt. Whether or not they did so, it is certain that someone struck a fleuron from his crown during the fight and that a battle-axe dented his helmet which can still be seen, to attest the fact, above his tomb in Westminster Abbey.

⚜

For half an hour the fighting went on as ferociously as it had begun; and at the end of that time in three places near where the King was fighting the piles of corpses and dying men were packed so high that they reached a level higher than the heads of the living. And the English soldiers clambered up on top of the great mounds to strike down at the still struggling figures beneath their feet or to drag out as prisoners those that looked most valuable.

Indeed, by now more men were gathering prisoners than were continuing the fight; and soon after midday there were, in fact, no Frenchmen left standing on the field to fight. In the distance the mounted men-at-arms of the third line still sat contemplating the disastrous scene, but they displayed no signs of attacking the victorious English army and some were already slinking away with the fugitives of the first two lines who had decided not to throw their lives away on so inglorious a field.

At one time during the morning—some reports place the incident much later—the Duke of Brabant, youngest brother of the Duke of Burgundy, made a strenuous effort to put new life into the dispirited army. He arrived late on the field with a few breathless followers after the battle had begun, and so anxious was he to join it—although his brother (who spent the day of the battle at a christening party) had ordered him not to do so—that he refused to wait for his servants to come up with his armour and instead borrowed his chamberlain's. Then, rallying what supporters would follow him, he charged through the mud towards the enemy. Stopping on the way to snatch a banner from a trumpet, he cut a hole in it and pulled it over his head as a surcoat. Tying another banner to his spear and shouting 'Brabant! Brabant!' he struggled forward on his way, followed by a few loyal men who were far from enough to save him from being knocked down and immediately captured.

The Englishmen at whom the Duke had so energetically charged, more surprised than alarmed by the diversion, returned to their more profitable activities of sorting out the living from the dead and from those so badly wounded that they might be discarded as worthless, of collecting and exchanging prisoners, arranging for ransoms and searching for loot.

For more than two hours this work went on, until prisoners worth thousands of pounds had been satisfactorily impounded. Throughout this time the King and his advisers had been keeping an eye on the mounted men-at-arms of the third French line, who, while making no threatening movements, yet still showed no signs of riding off. And they had been watching as well the groups of men-at-arms and bowmen of the first two lines, scattered far and wide all over the field, who had retreated from the carnage but might even now reorganise themselves and return. For if these men did return, supported by the mounted men, the English troops would have to abandon their prisoners in order to withstand their assault. The prisoners, whose armour had not yet been removed, would then certainly pick up what weapons they could find and fall on their captors from behind.

It was a potentially dangerous situation which had within it the possibilities of defeat. Uncounted numbers of French men-at-arms had already been killed; but the living, however scattered and disorganised they were, still outnumbered the exhausted English army. So long as Henry could hope, though, that there were no leaders left capable of rallying the dismembered and dispirited French troops for a second assault, he could believe that the danger was suppositional rather than real.

But some time towards the middle of the afternoon it seemed possible that such leaders might be emerging. The problem had been to get so large and heterogeneous a force as the French army to act together at all, even at the beginning of the battle; and this problem had now been greatly increased. Charles d'Albret was dead; Marshal Boucicaut and the Dukes of Orléans and Bourbon were all captured. Men refused to serve under banners other than their own; knights declined to accept orders from other knights. Burgundians would not serve under Armagnacs, and Armagnacs would not serve under Burgundians. Groups of Bretons, Gascons and Poitevins refused to serve under either.

The example of the Duke of Brabant, however, had been inspiring and now two other knights—the Counts of Marle and Fauquemberghes, who, by threats and the force of strong personalities had succeeded in keeping 600 men-at-arms under their control—began to make preparations to lead a charge at the English forces.

At the same time a rabble of several hundred peasants, led by three knights, made a second raid on the already plundered baggage. Only a small baggage-guard had been provided, for the King could not spare more than a few men from the fighting line, and during the battle even these few had wandered away from their posts, unwilling to lose their opportunity of securing a prisoner. Several horses, a precious sword and crown, some gold, silver, and many jewels were stolen from the King's baggage, but the raid in itself was not, of course, a serious military setback.

The threat by the mounted men-at-arms in the English front was, however, potentially disastrous. And the King did not hesitate to meet it. Determined not to risk losing the victory which was so nearly his, he gave a relentless order: all prisoners must be killed instantly.

The English soldiers heard the order with dismay. It was not that they were more soft-hearted than their King, nor that they would not have appreciated the danger of allowing the prisoners to escape when they were called upon to withstand the attack of the threatening horsemen in their front. What concerned them so deeply was the thought of losing the ransom money which had been almost theirs. It was a greater sacrifice than they were prepared to make. Undeterred by their reluctance, which in some cases seems to have amounted to open refusal, the King threatened to hang any man who disobeyed his orders and, to ensure that they were put into effect, commanded an esquire and 200 archers to perform the task that any captors themselves declined to perform. The threat and the command were enough and soon 'all those noblemen of France were there killed in cold blood and cut in pieces, heads and faces, which was a fearful sight to see'. [D]

Unknown numbers of throats were cut. Some said that there were more men killed in this way than were killed in the fighting. Certainly only the most valuable and distinguished prisoners—the Dukes of Orléans and Bourbon amongst them—were spared. The rest, as they stood, bareheaded but still in armour, in groups or alone, were cut or clubbed to death within a few minutes.

Even the houses to which some of the wounded had been taken by their comrades were set on fire so that none should escape. One knight, Gilbert de Lannoy, wounded in the head and the knee, managed to crawl out, however, and sold himself to Sir John Cornwall who eventually received 1,200 gold crowns and a good horse in ransom. But there were, evidently, few other survivors from the burning buildings.

The wholesale massacre was halted when it became clear that the threatened attack by the mounted men-at-arms, under Marle and Fauquemberghes, was unlikely to be more than a half-hearted diversion. But there were still a few isolated captives who were killed, even after the brave but unsupported French knights had trotted in disillusionment off the field. One of these was the pathetically quixotic Duke of Brabant, whose loyal retinue had left him on his own for fear that by crowding round him in his captivity they would draw attention to his rank and riches. His captor had removed his helmet, but seeing nothing in his features, nor in the eccentric makeshift surcoat he was wearing over his borrowed armour, to indicate the value of his prize, had decided he was not worth preserving and cut his throat.

❦

Henry V's 'cruel butchery' of his prisoners, as Sir James Ramsay described it in the nineteenth century, has been variously interpreted. According to René Belleval, also writing in the nineteenth century, '*les chevaliers pleuraient en pensant au déshonneur que cette horrible exécution allait faire rejaillir sur eux*'. It was '*barbare*', '*une boucherie*', '*une résolution inouïe*', '*elle restera imprimée comme une tache indélébile sur la réputation du héros d'Angleterre*'. And other later writers, both French and English, have taken up Belleval's complaint. Later, however, there has been an attempt to look at the King's action not with the eyes and mind of the modern humanitarian but with those of the early fifteenth-century knight, chivalrous yet relentless, idealistic yet practical, conscious of the mercy of Jesus, implacable as Jehovah. And there can certainly be no doubt that Henry's contemporaries did not condemn him. Even the French chroniclers write of his action as though it were dictated by painful necessity. They seem to imply that their leaders would have done the same in similar circumstances. Indeed, as Colonel Burne has pointed out, they had already done so twenty years before on the eve of the battle of Nicopolis when 1,000 prisoners were killed so that the army would not have to bother with them the next day.

Some French chroniclers go so far as to blame their own countrymen for the tragedy; and one speaks of the last attempt by the leaders of the third line to reopen the battle as 'an accursed assembling of wicked men' [D], disgracefully presumptuous in daring to attack the enemy when most of their great lords were captured or otherwise *hors de combat*.

King Henry, in fact, his enemies agreed, was not to be condemned; and his own disappointed soldiers could find it in their hearts to forgive him, no doubt, when looking across the field littered with the debris and splashed with the blood of battle, they could see the road to Calais, now open, stretching out of sight.

After the Battle

Crist that is our hevene Kyng,
His body and soule save and se.
Now all Ingelond may say and syng,
'Blessyd mote be the Trinitie.'
This jornay have ye herd how all be dene,
The date of Crist I wot it was,
A thousand foure hundred and fyftene.
     Wot ye right well that thus it was.
     Gloria tibi trinitas!

⚜

Where is the number of our English dead?
Edward the Duke of York, the Earl of Suffolk,
Sir Richard Ketly, Davy Gam, esquire:
None else of name; and of all other men
But five and twenty. O God, thy arm was here;
And not to us, but to thy arm alone,
Ascribe we all! When, without stratagem,
But in plain shock and even play of battle,
Was ever known so great and little loss
On one part and on th' other? Take it, God,
For it is none but thine!

Jamais désastre aussi grand n'avait été infligé à la France [wrote René de Belleval]. *Courtray, Crécy et Poitiers étaient surpassés. Parmi les princes et grands feudataires tués, on comptait le connétable Charles d'Albret, Jacques de Châtillon, seigneur de Dampierre, amiral de France; le Sire de Rambures, maître des arbalétriers: Guichard Dauphin, grand-maître d'hôtel du roi; Antoine, duc de Brabant, le duc Édouard de Bar, le duc d'Alençon, le comte de Nevers, Robert de Bar, comte de Marle; Ferry de Lorraine, comte de Vaudémont; Jean de Bar, Sire de Puisaye; le comte de Blamont, les comtes de Granpré, de Roucy et de Fauquemberghes, Louis de Bourdon. . . .*

The list goes on for ten pages. The total number of French dead can never be known. Contemporary estimates ranged from 4,000 to 11,000; a modern French historian has settled for 7,000; the most recent English historian for 10,000. A figure somewhere between these two last is probably correct. In addition, there were between 1,500 and 1,600 prisoners, all of them noblemen. Amongst these, in addition to Marshal Boucicaut and the Dukes of Orléans and Bourbon, were the Counts of Richemont, Eu and Vendôme.

In contrast the English casualties were negligible. The highest estimates put them at no more than 500 in all, and more reliable ones at 100; and most of these were wounded. The most distinguished of the dead were the Duke of York, whose unwounded but fat and suffocated body was pulled out from beneath one of the piles of steel-encased corpses, the young Earl of Suffolk, whose father had died of dysentery a few weeks before at Harfleur, Sir Richard Kyghley, Thomas Fitzhenry, John de Peniton, Walter Lord and Dafydd ap Llewelyn ap Hywel (David Gamme) who was knighted by the King as he lay dying.

The battle had lasted for about three hours and for the rest of the day the English soldiers roamed over the field, looking for still breathing noblemen amongst the piled heaps of corpses, knocking the armour off dead bodies and stripping them of the clothes and jewels beneath.

The King walked amongst them with several knights. For him it was not a personal victory, but God's triumph. The French, he said afterwards, had been hampered by their bad tactics and their ill discipline; but it was God who had allowed him to take such dreadful advantage of these faults. Some French apologists spoke of treachery, mentioning the names of both Charles d'Albret and the Duke of Orléans, and others of a curse upon their arms for allowing them to be directed by Armagnacs. Henry, though, saw the hand of God over all, remorselessly punishing his enemies for opposing the justice of England's cause. There were those of his soldiers who had beheld a vision of St George in the sky above their heads. Henry had never doubted that St George would be there.

He called for Montjoie, the Principal Herald of France, and in the presence of his own heralds asked him formally whether the victory belonged to him or to the King of France, reminding him that the slaughter was not of his doing but had been forced upon him by the intractability of Montjoie's countrymen. The French herald conceded the victory and Henry asked him the name of the Castle he saw beyond the woods to the north-west. Montjoie told him and the King said, 'Then, as all battles should bear the name of the fortress nearest to the field on which they are fought, this shall for ever be called the Battle of Agincourt.' [D]

⚜

Towards evening it began to rain again, and, there being no sign of any hostile movements from the enemy, the King ordered his army back to Maisoncelles.

The soldiers returned to the village with quantities of weapons, clothing and armour. They had stripped the bodies of the dead and wounded so thoroughly that they had left them as naked 'as when they came from their mother's womb' [D], or 'with covering only in the secret parts of nature'. [A]

To escape such treatment from the English during daylight and from the peasants who were to swarm on to the battlefield when it was dark, many of the wounded had managed to crawl away into the woods and ditches, but there most of them died. Only the English wounded and the rich were taken back to Maisoncelles.

The amount of armour that was brought back to the village was immense, for the English soldier, like every other soldier, has always had a passion for loot, however cumbersome or useless. And the King was obliged to give orders that no man should take more armour than he could wear himself, and that all the additional horse-loads that had come in and were still coming into the village were to be taken to a large barn on the outskirts of Maisoncelles where all the English dead had been placed. When it was full, the barn was set on fire, and it went on burning all night. The only corpses known to have been preserved from the holocaust were those of the Duke of York and the Earl of Suffolk. These were boiled so that the flesh might more easily be stripped from the bones which were to be taken back to England for burial.

At supper in the King's quarters that night the most distinguished of his prisoners waited at his table.

⚜

Outside on the battlefield the heaps of greyish-white blood-smeared corpses, stripped now of clothes and armour, lay still in the mud. Some bodies had been taken away by servants and had been washed before being carried home to their estates for burial; and there were many others, unknown or unrecognisable, that were taken up to the churchyards at Agincourt and Ruisseauville to be buried there when it was light—so many others, in fact, that two days later orders had to be given that no more could come for there was no more room for them. But most of the dead remained where they had fallen, their clotted scars covered with earth, their arms and thighs gnawed by wolves, their eyes pecked out by birds. At last, three pits were dug twelve feet wide and twenty-five yards long and into these 5,800 bodies were tipped. Each pit was marked by a large wooden cross and surrounded by a fence of thorns to keep out the wolves and dogs. In 1734 the Marchioness of Tramecourt vowed that if her son returned from the wars in Italy she would build a chapel on the site where his ancestors had died. He did return and the chapel was built. In the Revolution, sixty years later, however, it was destroyed and its materials used for pigsties.

There is another memorial there now, built by the present proprietor of the land in memory of yet other ancestors who were killed there and of his own sons who also fought for France over these sad fields where soldiers have been dying for more than a thousand years.

❧

During the morning of 26 October the English troops, no longer in *côtes d'armes*, set out for Calais with their prisoners, passing over the field of battle where a few wounded and naked Frenchmen were still surprisingly alive. The poor and those who could not walk were killed; the rest added to the number of prisoners.

Despite the King's orders that no excessive armour was to be taken on the march, each man had as much with him as he could possibly carry. And the army's own horses and those that had been captured from the French were also weighed down with loads of plunder, most of it military equipment, *faute de mieux*. The going was slow—about eleven miles a day—for the men were excessively tired as well as overloaded and many of them had prisoners or wounded men to find food for and it was difficult enough finding food for themselves. Hunger and exhaustion brought on depression, and the high spirits that had elated the army after their victory evaporated in the cold, damp air.

The King's mood, however, remained unaltered. Apparently he spent much of the time on the march talking to his prisoners. He treated them well, sending them bread and wine from his own table; but his conversation, as recorded by more than one chronicler, cannot have been other than tiresome.

'Noble cousin, be of good heart', he is reported to have said, with what sounds to the modern ear distressingly unctuous and complacent piety, to the Duke of Orléans.

'I know that God gave me the victory over the French, not that I deserved it. But I fully believe that he wished to punish my enemies; and that, if what I have heard be true, it is not to be wondered at, for

Thomas, Lord Camoys and his wife
From a church brass at Trotton, Sussex

never were there greater disorders, sensuality and vices seen than
now prevail in France, which it is horrible to hear described. And if
God is provoked, no one can be surprised by it.' [D]

Nor can we be surprised that the Duke of Orléans and the other
noble prisoners avoided the King's company as much as they could.
When the army reached Guisnes, however, they were less often able
to do so, for at the castle here Henry decided to stay with them for a
while, leaving his mean to go on to Calais alone.

Their arrival there was a cruel disappointment. Expecting to be
welcomed as conquerors, to be fêted and fed, most of them could not
even find lodgings, and some, though 'greatly distressed by famine
and other wants' [D], were not even allowed to pass through the
gates of the town. A large supply of cattle and pigs, salted fish, flour
and beer had been sent over for them from London; but it had not
yet arrived, and the inhabitants of Calais were unwilling to part with
provisions of their own, or, being persuaded to do so, demanded
such inflated prices for them that the soldiers were obliged to sell
their baggage, their plunder and their prisoners.

Hundreds of prisoners changed hands in Calais or bought their
freedom for a far smaller ransom than their captors can have hoped,
even in their most pessimistic moments, to receive for them.

Several days passed before ships arrived from Dover and Sandwich to take the English soldiers home and as they waited in idle-
ness a rumour went round the army that they would not yet be
going home at all, as the King had other plans for them.

Henry had come into the town in triumph on the afternoon of
29 October. He had been escorted by the Captain of Calais, the Earl
of Warwick, the leading citizens and merchants who had gone almost
as far as Guisnes to meet him, and by priests and chaplains in their
richest canonicals chanting the *Te Deum Laudamus*. As he had entered
through the gates, the women and children of the town had dutifully
sung 'Welcome to the King, our Sovereign Lord!'

Conscious of having won a great and decisive victory, the King
was reluctant to let his troops go home without having followed it
up. Had the men not been so worn out at Agincourt, he might perhaps have succeeded in advancing on Paris and entering it, for the
only army that France had in the field had been utterly dispersed.
That opportunity had had to be abandoned; but he might, he

thought, even now employ his men on some less spectacular operation before sending them home. He suggested to his War Council an attack on various strongholds outside the Calais Pale, and mentioned in particular Ardres. The suggestion aroused the strongest opposition in the Council and while he was able to override his Councillors after the fall of Harfleur, he could not, or did not, attempt to do so now; and he gave way to their advice.

On 11 November the Sire d'Estouteville, the Sire de Gaucourt, and the other prisoners taken at Harfleur gave themselves up to him as they had promised to do; and at the end of the following week, a 'prosperous gale' having blown up, he embarked for home.

For his prisoners it was a fearful voyage. Unaccustomed to the rolling of a ship, even in a gentle sea, they suffered agonies of seasickness during a crossing that proved to be so unusually boisterous that some ships were driven into the port of Zierickzee in Holland, before being able to resume their voyage. Most of the prisoners, moreover, had already been in great distress of spirit before they had embarked, for none of them could know when they would see France again.

Several of them, bought by merchants in Calais, had been sold outright as servants to noble families or ecclesiastical orders, and were on their way to various great houses and abbeys in England from which there could be little prospect of escape. Others were charged with ransoms that would burden their families for life and would take months and perhaps years to raise. Few could look forward to an early return. And for some, even of the most distinguished, there was to be no return.

Marshal Boucicaut and the Duke of Bourbon were two of those who died in England, unable to pay the heavy ransoms the English King demanded of them. The Duke of Orléans was still in England in 1436, having been imprisoned at Windsor, Pomfret Castle and the Tower; and was not permitted to return to France until he had sworn on the Sacrament in the presence of Henry VI that he would never bear arms against England again.

Perhaps, though, even the prospect of long years of exile and confinement in England was not so appalling to these men as they lay on board ship, suffering violent seasickness for the first time, as was the immediate fear that they would never feel dry land again.

And, in the meantime, an indignity more immediate than captivity was to be undergone: they would be required to form part of the victory parade in London.

⚜

The news of Agincourt had reached London on 29 October, the day Henry reached Calais, and Bishop Beaufort, the Chancellor, had read out the news from the steps of St Paul's. The rejoicing had been instantaneous and in every church the bells had pealed until sunset.

Over a fortnight had gone by since then and the people had been awaiting the King's return in growing excitement. Then on 15 November came the news that his ship was beating about outside Dover harbour.

The following day, although it was still blowing hard and snowing heavily, a vast crowd collected on the beach to welcome him. As he drew close to the shore in a longboat, the Barons of the Cinque Ports waded into the ice-cold sea and, lifting him out, carried him on to the shingle. The people greeted him 'with frantic shouts of joy'.

Homecoming

To London brigge thanne roode oure Kyng,
The processions there, they mette hym ryght,
'Ave Rex Anglos' thei gan syng
'Flos mundi' thei seyde, Goddys Knyght
To London brigge whan he com ryght,
Upon the gate ther stode on hy,
A gyaunt that was full grym of syght,
To teche the Frensshmen curtesye.
    Wot ye right well that thus it was.
    Gloria tibi trinitas!

⚜

Thus far, with rough and all-unable pen,
Our bending author hath pursued the story,
In little room confining mighty men,
Mangling by starts the full course of their glory.
Small time, but in that small most greatly lived
This star of England: Fortune made his sword;
By which the world's best garden he achieved,
And of it left his son imperial lord.

IO

As on landing in France, so now on returning home the King knelt in prayer. He prayed on the beach at Dover and at Canterbury he prayed at the shrine of St Thomas and kissed the Cathedral's holy relics. God had brought him his victory. With God's help he would strive to be worthy of it.

Travelling by way of Eltham, he set out for London on the morning of 23 November. At Blackheath he was met by the new Lord Mayor, Nicholas Wolton (known as 'Witless Nick' in the city), twenty-four aldermen and thousand upon thousand of citizens and craftsmen, all dressed in scarlet and wearing the devices of their companies. The Mayor formally congratulated the King on the great victory that he had won, and then the long cavalcade rode off towards Southwark and London.

For days the city had been preparing a welcome worthy of so magnificent a victor; and as he entered it by way of the gatehouse at the Stoops by London Bridge Henry could see how triumphal his greeting was to be.

On either side of the gatehouse, at the top of its two towers, a gigantic statue had been erected. One of these figures 'of amazing magnitude' was of a sentinel who held a battle-axe in his right hand and offered the King the keys of the city in his left. By his side stood a female figure, almost as immense, clothed in a scarlet cloak and decorated with jewels and sparkling ornaments. All around both figures, banners and standards flew in the wind from the turrets of the towers, while 'trumpets, clarions and horns sounded in various melody'.

The King and his retinue stood still for a moment, wondering at the sight and sound of their welcome. Then the King said in a loud voice, 'Hail to the royal city!' and they went on towards the bridge.

They passed between two tall wooden columns covered with linen painted to represent blocks of white marble and green jasper. Looking up towards the top of the column on their right, they saw the figure of an antelope with the royal arms hanging on a shield from his neck and with the royal sceptre grasped between the paws of his right forefoot; and turning to the left they saw a lion holding a staff from which hung the royal standard.

Beyond the bridge they came towards an immense arch raised across the street, and on top of the arch, inside a pavilion of crimson tapestry, there was a statue of St George in armour, his helmet covered with a laurel wreath studded with pearls and precious stones. And as they passed beneath the arch, 'innumerable boys, representing the angelic host, arrayed in white with their faces painted gold and with glittering wings and virgin locks set with precious sprigs of laurel, sang in melodious voices to the sound of organs an English anthem:

> Owre Kynge went forth to Normandy,
> With grace and myght of chivalry;
> The God for hym wrought marvelously,
> Wherefore Englonde may calle, and cry
> > Deo gratias:
> Deo gratias Anglia redde pro victoria.
>
> He sette a sege, the soothe for to say,
> To Harfleur toune with royal array;
> That toun he wan, and made a fray,
> That Fraunce shall rywe tyl domes day.
> > Deo gratias:
> Deo gratias Anglia redde pro victoria.
>
> Then went oure Kynge, with alle his oste,
> Thorowe Fraunce for all the French boste;
> He spared 'nor' drede of leste, ne moste,
> Tyl he come to Agincourt coste.
> > Deo gratias:
> Deo gratias Anglia redde pro victoria.
>
> Then for sothe that Knyghte comely,
> In Agincourt feld he faught manly;
> Thorow grace of God most myghty,
> He had both the felde, and the victory.
> > Deo gratias:
> Deo gratias Anglia redde pro victoria.

Ther dukys, and erlys, lorde and barone,
Were take, and slayne, and that wel done,
And some were ledde into Lundone,
With joye, and merthe and grete renone.
                              Deo gratias:
Deo gratias Anglia redde pro victoria.

Now gracious God he save oure kynge,
His peple, and all his well wyllnge,
Gef him gode lyfe, and gode endynge,
That we with merth mowe savely synge
                              Deo gratias:
Deo gratias Anglia redde pro victoria.

The procession wound up Fish Hill through the Cornmarket in Grass Church towards the rough and narrow streets that stretched from Leadenhall to St Paul's. At the Tun in Cornhill, there was another tower draped in crimson cloth, the hem of the cloth held out on long red poles in representation of an open tent. As the King passed by the tent and looked inside,

a company of prophets, of venerable hoariness, dressed in golden coats and mantles, with their heads covered and wrapped in gold and crimson, sent forth a great quantity of sparrows and little birds, as a sacrifice agreeable to God in return for victory. Some birds alighted on the King's breast, some rested on his shoulders, and some fluttered round about him. And the prophets sang with sweet harmony, bowing to the ground, this psalm of thanksgiving: '*Cantate Domino canticum novum, Alleluia! Quia mirabilia fecit, Alleluia!*'

On through Cheapside, past vast tapestries on which were worked scenes representing the deeds of English heroes, past great banners and standards, escutcheons and shields, flags fluttering on velvet-covered poles, by miniature forts and linen-covered castles that 'seemed to grow out of the buildings' on either side, beneath damask awnings and arches of halberds that stretched from roof to roof above their heads, the King and his friends and his awestruck prisoners went towards St Paul's.

Here, on one side of the Cathedral, were more old men 'having the names of the twelve apostles written on their foreheads, together with the twelve Kings, Martyrs and Confessors of the succession of England, their loins girded with golden sceptres, sceptres also in their hands and crowns on their heads, chanting with one accord at the King's approach'. And there, on the other side, were raised pavilions filled with 'most beautiful virgin girls, standing motionless like statues, decorated with very elegant ornaments of modesty and crowned with laurel and girt with golden girdles, having in their hands cups of gold from which they blew, with gentle breath scarcely perceptible, round leaves of gold upon the King's head as he passed beneath them'. And in front by the steps of the Cathedral itself, more beautiful girls, clothed all in white, came out towards him, 'singing with timbrel and dance, this song of congratulation: *'Welcome, Henry the Fifte, Kynge of Englond and of Fraunce'*; while little boys, also dressed in white, their hair covered in jewels, threw down from the towers of a 'very fair castle made of wood with no less ingenuity than elegance', gilt wavers and laurel leaves.

And everywhere,

> besides the pressure in the standing places, and of people crowding through the streets, and the multitudes of men and women looking through openings and apertures, the lattices and windows on both sides were filled with the most noble ladies and women of the realm and with honourable and honoured men who flocked together to the wonderful sight and were so very gracefully and elegantly dressed in fine garments of gold and crimson and various other apparel, that a greater assembly or a more splendid spectacle was not recollected to have been seen in London ever before. [A]

The King himself, amidst all the excitement and the adulation, passed quietly along in a purple robe, modest and thoughtful. He had been pressed to wear the helmet that had been battered by the axe at Agincourt, but he insisted on walking through the crowds bareheaded and on foot. He had few attendants with him, and often he was obliged to wait patiently while they cleared a path for him through the crowds. When men raised their voices to praise him extravagantly, he asked them not to praise him but God.

At the door of St Paul's he was greeted by eighteen bishops in their pontificals, and he followed them to the High Altar where he sank humbly to his knees.

⚜

The character of this remarkable man has long puzzled historians. To his English contemporaries he was '*sans peur et sans reproche*', a 'noble prince and victoriouse Kynge, floure in his tyme of Cristen chivalrie', a 'Julius in intellect, a Hector in valour, an Achilles in strength, an Augustus in morals, a Paris in eloquence, a Solomon in dialectic, and a Troilus in love', 'al nobleness, manhode and vertue', 'felicitous in all things'.

Even French contemporaries, who had little good to say of English people, could not but admire their King. He was 'above all the prince of justice, both in relation to himself for the sake of example, and in relation to others, according to equity and right; he gave support to none out of favour, nor did he suffer wrong to go unpunished out of regard for kinship.'

It was an opinion which Shakespeare's contemporaries endorsed. They recognised in *King Henry V* a noble soldier, selfless, brave, patriotic, honourable, human and just, the 'true monarch of Eliza-bethan idealism', as Professor Jacob has put it, 'a figure dominant over State and Church alike, an instrument of the divine will'.

To a people who looked back on his time as a golden age, Henry was, indeed, 'this star of England'. Fortune made his sword. He possessed all the virtues of the good mediaeval king. His piety, his courage, his sense of justice and his brilliant generalship were all unquestioned. His supposedly wild youth added a pleasing touch of humanity to his stern nobility.

In more recent years this unqualified approval of the paragon of paladins has not been found acceptable. Was there not much that was unfeeling and bigoted in the strict morality of his adult life, much that was priggish and sanctimonious in his piety, deceitful in his diplomacy, selfish in his patriotism, secretive in his reserve? He may have been a great soldier but he was a hard, domineering and, on occasions, cruel man. It was remembered that as a young prince of twenty-three, five years before the battle of Agincourt, he had supervised the burning of a blacksmith who had maintained that the Sacrament was not the body and blood of Christ; that during the battle itself he had ordered the slaughter of unknown numbers of defenceless prisoners in the face of a threat which turned out to be a false alarm; and that three years after the battle, while besieging Rouen, he had refused to let 12,000 old men, women and children—*bouches inutiles*—pass through his lines during the cruel severities of an appalling winter in which most of them died. Rouen was his own city, it was withheld from him against all justice and God's will. He would not bargain with them.

The tremor of distaste is inevitable. But the King was a man of his age, and it is the age, which by the modern liberal conscience, must be condemned as distasteful. Henry V may have been more concerned with the future of the House of Lancaster than with that of the Kingdom of England; he may have been less concerned with the conquest of France as a step to the conquest of the Infidel than he pretended; he may have been more of an adventurer than a statesman; he may have had many, if not all, of the faults of character that have reliably been attributed to him. But he was still the greatest Englishman of his time. He was also England's greatest soldier.

This reputation as the greatest soldier his country produced in the fifteenth century owes more, perhaps, than is usually suggested, to many leading officers in his army whose names are for the most part forgotten. Several of them, like himself, had served a long apprenticeship to arms in Wales, others had gathered experience on the Scottish border or in France. And some of them could, no doubt, with a King's authority behind them, have led an experienced and well-trained army to success. Apart from the royal dukes, the parts played by such men as Sir John Holland, Sir John Cornwall, Sir Gilbert Umfraville, Sir Thomas Erpingham, Lord Camoys and Dafydd ap Llewelyn in the Agincourt campaign have long been overlooked. To do justice to the abilities and influence of men like these and to the courage of the men-at-arms and archers under their command is not to suggest, of course, that Henry's high reputation as a leader is undeserved.

He brought to the direction of his army a special quality of leadership that was as rare as it was effective. His men admired his dash and spirit, the energy and stamina, the force and determination, the verve and panache of the ideal mediaeval knight. It was in these qualities that his greatness lay. He was not a powerful-looking man, but he was lithe and athletic and he wore his armour 'as though it were a light cloak'. His features, an apparently accurate reflection of his musical and liturgical tastes, were more those of a monk or an intellectual than those of the fighting soldier; but he *was* a fighting soldier. And his troops recognised him as one. He shared their hardships; he spoke to them in words they could understand. He was a king but he showed that he understood the feelings and aspirations of common men. He was not excitable, neither wildly elated in victory nor obviously dismayed by defeat, and he never gave way to hysteria or panic. His calm and contemplative eyes became terrifying when he was angry, but his anger did not rise without good cause. He was stern, relentless, even implacable but his soldiers found him just and he was a man of his word; he succeeded in imparting to them much of his own dedicated enthusiasm and moral fervour. They grumbled when he refused to allow them to plunder, but they respected him and most of them obeyed him. He was masterful, decisive and competent with a sense of authority that was at once impressive and reassuring. He was, in short, a natural leader of men.

So much is undoubted. Whether or not he was a great general is, however, a question which requires investigation. He owed much to luck, of course—but then all successful generals have done; he made mistakes—they all do that; he profited as much from his enemies' blunders as from his own unerring decisions—few do not. Beyond these considerations, there is, though, an element of doubt about his capacity as a general which an examination of his strategy and tactics during the Agincourt campaign—and his later campaigns were almost entirely limited to sieges—does nothing to dispel.

To describe his determination to march on Calais after the fall of Harfleur as 'the most foolhardy and reckless adventure that ever an unreasoning pietist devised', as Dr J. H. Wylie did, is no doubt an unjust exaggeration. For there are good grounds for believing that Henry fully recognised the dangers that such an adventure entailed; and that he discounted them only after a careful and perhaps inspired consideration of the enemy's likely reactions. His reliance on French dissensions was, however, only partly justified as, although he was right in believing that the Duke of Burgundy would continue to procrastinate, he did not allow for the fact that Marshal Boucicaut's suspicion of the Duke might—as in fact it did—lead to French forces advancing quickly across Burgundian territory to the north bank of the Somme.

Even so, leaving aside his faith in God's guidance and help, Henry's *chevauchée* across the Somme through Picardy might, perhaps, more accurately be termed, in Colonel Burne's phrase, 'a justifiable and commendable risk', than a 'foolhardy and reckless adventure'. To set out, however, for the Blanche-Taque ford on the Somme without ensuring that it would still be open when he arrived there was a mistake which involved a long, painful and dangerous march that could have been disastrous. He did instruct the Captain of Calais to send a force down towards the Somme, but he did not himself send forward an advance-guard or even a reconnaissance party, to discover whether or not the troops from Calais had succeeded in their task, although he had eight days—while awaiting the Dauphin's answer to his challenge—in which to do so. And it was consequently not until he had crossed the Bresle and was coming down towards the Somme estuary that he learned that the small force of 300 men that had been sent down from Calais by Sir William Bardolf had been driven back long before it reached the Blanche-Taque ford, which was by then guarded by a strong French force.

The march eastwards towards the boggy headwaters of the Somme was now inevitable; and it was only after the army had reached Fouilly that Henry learned—not from his own scouts, apparently, but first from prisoners of war and then from intimidated peasants anxious to get rid of so many hungry men—of a suitable crossing place. The immediate change of direction across the downland from Fouilly to Voyennes and Béthencourt, since it enabled him to cross the river without interference by the French army which until then had been shadowing him, has been described as a 'brilliant step on the part of the English King', though it seems, in fact, if not actually forced on him by necessity, more adventitious than adroit.

The subsequent seventy-mile march from Athies to Agincourt was undoubtedly a tribute to the endurance and discipline of Henry's army, but the French troops—most of whom had already come heavily equipped with both guns and wagons a hundred miles from Rouen, and some of whom had come much further, and were not all mounted—went by a longer route and got there before him to close the road to Calais. It cannot, I think, be doubted that up to this stage of the campaign Henry was out-generalled.

Nothing, however, succeeds like a victory. And whether or not Henry's triumph owed more to the obsolete tactics of the French army and the reckless and insubordinate behaviour of the French men-at-arms than to his own prowess, it *was* a great triumph. The results of the campaign—limited as they were to the possession of

Harfleur—a doubtful asset—and the acquisition of ransom money, cannot be said to be impressive. Nor can it be denied that Normandy could have been conquered later, had Agincourt never been fought. But the whole Christian world was impressed and the prestige that Henry had acquired made it possible for him to return to France as a feared and respected conqueror.

Henry went back in the summer of 1417 with hopes of recovering Normandy and extending his possessions in south-western France. He laid siege to Caen and it fell without a struggle; the Duke of Gloucester entered Bayeux unresisted; Falaise surrendered at the beginning of January 1418. Rouen offered stronger resistance, but that too fell to the English a year later; and with its fall came the conquest of Normandy. In the following year the Treaty of Troyes was signed and Henry was made heir and regent of France and married Catherine, the King's daughter. The leadership of all Christendom was now within his grasp and his thoughts turned once more to a new crusade against the Infidel. But his health broke down in the summer of 1422 and on 31 August at the age of thirty-four he died at Vincennes.

When he lay dying, as though answering unspoken charges, he justified his attack on France:

> 'It was not ambitious lust for dominion, nor for empty glory, nor any other cause, that drew me to these wars, but only that by suing of my right, I might at once gain peace and my own rights. . . . And before the wars were begun I was fully instructed by men of the holiest life and the wisest counsel that I ought and could with this intention begin the wars, prosecute them, and justly finish them without danger to my soul.'

Later he interrupted his confessor and chaplains, who were saying with him the psalms of penance, and added:

> 'O Good Lord, thou knowest that, if thy pleasure had been to have suffered me to live my natural age, my firm purpose and intent was, after I had established this realm of France in sure peace, to have gone and visited Jerusalem and to have re-edified the walls thereof, and to have repulsed from it the miscreants, thine adversaries.'

It was for this ultimate purpose he now felt sure, and, perhaps, always had felt sure, that the battle of Agincourt had been fought. But it was not God's will that he should fulfil that purpose.

He died to leave his country in the care of a regent and a baby-king who eventually, not having his powers of leadership or his degree of parliamentary support, and having to contend with the rising force of French national pride and its inspired epitome, Joan of Arc, was to lose all for which his father had fought.

Genealogical Table
of the Kings of France
and England

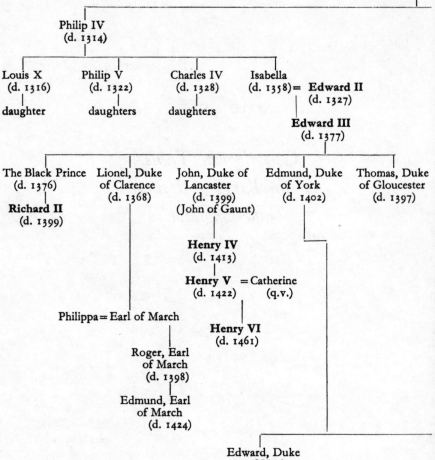

Philip III
(d. 1285)

Philip IV
(d. 1314)

Louis X
(d. 1316)
daughter

Philip V
(d. 1322)
daughters

Charles IV
(d. 1328)
daughters

Isabella
(d. 1358) = **Edward II**
(d. 1327)

Edward III
(d. 1377)

The Black Prince
(d. 1376)
Richard II
(d. 1399)

Lionel, Duke
of Clarence
(d. 1368)

John, Duke of
Lancaster
(d. 1399)
(John of Gaunt)

Edmund, Duke
of York
(d. 1402)

Thomas, Duke
of Gloucester
(d. 1397)

Henry IV
(d. 1413)

Henry V = Catherine
(d. 1422)   (q.v.)

Philippa = Earl of March

Henry VI
(d. 1461)

Roger, Earl
of March
(d. 1398)

Edmund, Earl
of March
(d. 1424)

Edward, Duke
of York
(d. at Agincourt, 1415)

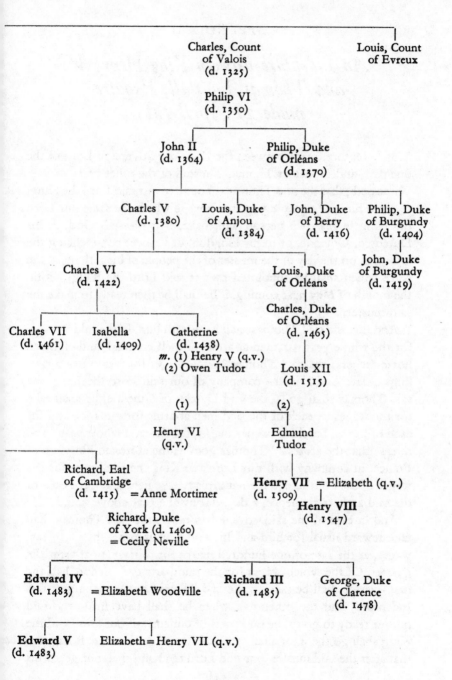

An Indenture between King Henry V and Thomas Tunstall, Esquire made 29 April 1415

This Indenture, made between the King our Sovereign Lord of the one part, and Monsieur Thomas Tunstall of the other part: Witnesseth, that the said Thomas is bound to our said Lord the King, to serve him for a whole year in a voyage which the same our Lord the King in his own person will make, if it pleaseth God, in his Dutchy of Guienne, or in his kingdom of France: commencing the said year, on the day of the muster of the people of his retinue, at the place which shall be appointed by our said Lord the King, within the month of May next coming, if he shall be then ready to make the said muster.

And that the said Thomas shall have with him, in the said voyage, for the whole year, six men-at-arms, himself counted, and eighteen horse archers; the said Thomas taking wages for himself two shillings a day. And if in the company of our said Lord the King, the said Thomas shall go to the said Dutchy of Guienne, he shall take for the wages of each of the said men-at-arms forty marks, and for each of the said archers twenty marks, for the said whole year. And in case that the aforesaid Thomas goes to the aforesaid kingdom of France, in company with our Lord the King, he shall take for the wages of each of the said men-at-arms twelve-pence, and for each of the said archers six-pence, a day, during the year above said.

And in case of the said voyage to France, the said Thomas shall take reward usual for him and his said men-at-arms, that is to say, wages, at the rate of one hundred marks for thirty men-at-arms the quarter. Of the which wages for the said parts of Guienne, half the first quarter shall be paid to the said Thomas at the making of this Indenture; and the other half when he shall have made the said muster ready to go to the said parts of Guienne, if our said Lord the King shall go there, or shall send him there. And in case it happens that after the said muster, our said Lord the King shall not go to his said Dutchy of Guienne, but shall go to the parts of France, then the said Thomas shall be paid so much as shall be owing to him for the said first quarter, besides the sum received by him as above, for the wages and reward, as well for himself as for the men-at-arms and archers above said, so passing to the said parts of France.

And for surety of payment for the second quarter, our said Lord the King will cause to be delivered to the said Thomas, in pledge, on the first day of June next coming, Jewels, which by agreement with the said Thomas, shall be fully worth the sum to which the said wages, or wages with reward, for that quarter shall amount. The which jewels the said Thomas shall be bound to return to our said Lord the King, the hour that he can redeem them within a year and half and one month next after the receipt of the same jewels.

And also that it shall be lawful for the said Thomas and for all others whatsoever, to whom the said jewels shall be delivered by the said Thomas, after the end of the said month, to dispose of the said jewels at their pleasure, without impeachment of the King or of his heirs, according to the contents of the Letters Patent, under the Great Seal of the King, granted to the aforesaid Thomas in this case. And for the third quarter, the said Thomas shall be paid for him and his said retinue, within six weeks after the commencement of the same third quarter, according to the quantity of wages, or wages with reward, for the country to which they may have gone, or shall be, during the said quarter.

And respecting the payment of the wages, or wages with reward, as the case may be, for the last quarter of the year above said, if for the moiety of the said third quarter, the King, our said Lord, shall not give such security for the payment to the said Thomas as he shall reasonably demand, then, at the expiration of the third quarter, the said Thomas shall be acquitted and discharged towards our said Lord the King of the covenants specified in this present Indenture. And the said Thomas shall be bound to be ready at the sea, with his said people well mounted, armed, and equipped, suitably to their condition, for his muster on the first day of July next coming: and from the time of their arrival at the place above said, the said Thomas is bound to muster the people of his retinue before such person or persons as it may please our said Lord the King to assign, as often as he shall reasonably require.

And the said Thomas shall have as usual at the charge of our said Lord, shipping for him and his retinue, their horses, harness, and provisions, and also re-shipping, as others of his condition in the said voyage. And if it shall happen, that our said Lord the King shall countermand the said Thomas before his passage of the sea, he shall be bound for the said sum to serve the same our Lord the King, in such parts as shall please him with the aforesaid men-at-arms and archers, according to the rate of wages accustomed in the parts where they shall be ordered by our said Lord the King, except those that may die, if any shall die, in the mean time.

And if it shall happen that the Adversary of France, or any of his sons, nephews, uncles, or cousin-germans, or any King of any kingdom, or his Lieutenant, or other chieftains having command from the said Adversary of France, shall be taken in the said voyage by the said Thomas, or any of his said retinue, our said Lord the King shall have the said Adversary, or other person of the rank above said, who may be so taken, and shall make reasonable agreement with the said Thomas, or to those by whom he may be taken. And respecting other profits of 'Gaignes de Guerre' our said Lord the King shall have as well the third part of the 'gaignes' of the said Thomas, as the third of the third part of the 'gaignes' of the people of his retinue in the said voyage taken, as the 'gaignes' of the prisoners, booty, money, and all gold, silver and jewels, exceeding the value of ten marks.

In Witness of which things on the part of this Indenture relating to our said Lord the King, the aforesaid Thomas has put his Seal. Given at Westminster, the xxix day of April, the year of the reign of our said Lord the King, the third.

[Translated from the French of Thomas Rymer's *Foedera, Conventiones, Literae et cujuscunque generis Acta Publica inter Reges Angliae, ix* (1709) and printed in Sir Harris Nicolas's *History of the Battle of Agincourt* (1832).]

APPENDIX III

The Retinue of King Henry V

As well as men-at-arms and archers, the King's retinue included these
specialist troops, tradesmen and members of his Household:

John Greyndon, Knight with Mynors 120

Gerard Van Willighen ⎫
Hans Joye ⎪
Walter Stotmaker ⎬ Master Gunners, with others . . 25
Drovankesell Coykyn ⎭

Each with 2 Servitour Gunners 50

Nicholas Brampton, Stuffer of Bacynets

Allbright Mailmaker ⎫
   with other ⎬ Armurers 12

Leicester ⎫
Guienne ⎬ King of Arms
Irlande ⎭

Hereford, Mareschal of Arms

Valletz Peyntours 4

John Covyn, Sergeant of the Kinge's Tents and Pavilons, with other
   Yomen of the Pavilons 28

Mr Nicholas Colnet, Phisitian, with 3 Archers

Thomas Morestede, and ⎫Surgeons⎧each with 9 ⎫
William Bradwardyn ⎭   ⎩more Surgeons⎭ . . 20

John Waterton, Esq., Master ⎫with Groomes . . . 60
   of the King's Horse ⎭

John Othvin, Yoman, Surveyour of the Stable

Nichol Harewode, Clerk of the Stable

Ranulph Apulton, Clerk of the King's Avenrie

William Grene Gerneter ⎫ with other yomen Purveyours . 12
William Medewey ⎭

Gerard de la Strade, Grome of the Horses

Guy Midelton and ⎫ the King's Guides by night
John Melton ⎭

Richard Hodel and ⎫ with Yomen Smiths 12
Thomas Smith ⎭

Richard Berre and other Sadlers ⎫ 9
   with Yomen Sadlers ⎭

Clerk of the Marshalcy

William Kynwolmersh, Cofferer of the King's Household

Mr William Smith, Esquire with Yomen 41

Thomas Harvy and other Servitours of the King 8

Griffith Percival, with other Yomen of the King 8

Thomas Tunbrigge } with other } Yomen of the King's Household . . 86

Robert Spore } with other } Yomen 13

William Heryot } with other } pages, Messengers of the King's Chamber . 3

Norman Synford } with other } Yomen of the King's Poultry . . . 3

Nicholas Burcestre } with other } Yomen of the Bakehouse 8

William Balne, Clerk of the Kitchin

Robert Allerton and } Richard Reston } Under Clerks of the Kitchin, Pantry and Buttery

Jacob Meyndy, Clerk, Yoman of the office of Napery

Wauter Burton and } John Langayle } Clerks of the Spicery

William Pek, under Clerk of the Spicery

John Hanham, Clerk of the Poultry

William Sharpeton, Clerk of the Scullery

John Canterbury, for the office of Scullery

Thomas Westerdale with Laborers } and Bowgemen for the } Scullery 15

John Desye, Clerk of the Bakehouse

John Breton, Clerk of the Hall

William Carpenter } with other } Carpenters of the Hall 6

Thomas Fysh } with other } Labourers of the Hall 19

John Waterton and } William Foster } Bowgemen

John Feriby } Thomas Morton } Clerks of the Wardrobe

William Topnel and others of the Wardrobe

William Topnel, Master Tayller, with 2 Archers

George Benet, Master Cordwaner } with other } Cordwaners 26

Thomas Matthew } William Temple } Master Carpenters with other Carpenters . 124

Robert Mitchell, with other Fletchers 6

Nicholas Frost, with other Bowyers 6

John Flete, with other Whelerights 6

John atte Herst } Robert Berton } Colliers

John Benet, with other Labourers 120
Estephin Payn, Almoigner
Thomas Bridde, Sub Almoigner
Master John de Bordin, Clerk, Doctor in Laws,
    with 1 Clerk, and 2 Archers
Richard Hals, Clerk, with 1 Clerk and 2 Archers
Master Esmon Lacy, Dean of the King's Chapel
John Burnell and ⎫
John Mildenhale ⎭ Chaplains of the King's Chapel
Master Stephen Morpath ⎫
    with other ⎭ Chaplains 13
Frere Alain Hert ⎫
Frere John Brotherton ⎭ with other of the Revestry . . . 14

MINSTRELS

John Cliff	Wauter Haliday
Thomas Norys Tromper	Meysham Pyper
William Baldewyn	Broune Pyper
John Michel	Snayth Fydler
Panel Trumper	William Langton
Peut Trumper	Thomas Hardiberd
Richard Pyper	William Halliday
Thomas Haliday	

[The names appear in Thomas Rymer's *Foedera, Conventiones, Literae et cujuscunque generis Acta Publica inter Reges Angliae* (1709), and were printed in full in Sir Harris Nicolas's *History of the Battle of Agincourt* (1832).]

King Henry V's Ordinances of War

⚜

THE STATUTES AND ORDINANCES TO BE
KEPT IN TIME OF WERRE

1. First, all manere of men, of what condicion or estate they be of, be obeyssant to our lorde the kynge, and his conestable and mareschalle, upon peyne of asmoche as they mow [may] forfetes in bodyes and goodes.

The peyne of hym that toucheth the sacrament

2. That no man be so hardy, o lesse than [unless] he be a prest, to touche the sacrament of Goddes body, upon peyne to be drawene and hanged, and that non other man touche the boxe or vesselle, in the whiche the precious sacrament is yn, unreverently, upon the same peyne above said.

The peyne of hym that robbeth holy chirche

3. That no man be so hardy to robbe ne pille holy chirche of no good ne ornament that longeth to the chirche, ne to slee no man of holy chirche religious ne order, byt yf he be armed, upon peyne of deth. Ne that no man be so hardy to slee ne enforce no woman, upon the same peyne, and that no man take prisonners woman, or man of holy chirche, ne other religious, but yf he be armed, upon peyne of prisonment and his body at the kyng wille.

No man shal goo before the oost outake [except]
herbergers [quartermasters], under peyne, &c.

4. Also that no man be so hardy to goo tofore beyng in bataille undre the baner or penon of his lord or maistre, except the kyng and other lordes herbergeours, the names of which shall be take and delivered by their lord or maistres unto the conestable and mareschalle, upon this peyne, that he that offendeth shalbe put from his horse bothe

unto the warde of the conestable and mareschalle, unto tyme that he
that so offendeth hath made fyne with them and found seurete that he
shall no more offende. Also no man shall logge hym selfe, but shall
be logged by the kynges herbergeour, and obey hym in that under
the same peyne.

No man after he is logged shal remove hym, under
the peyne above said

5. Also that no man take herbegage, but by assignement of conestable and mareschalle or of the herbergeours. And that after tyme
that the herbegage is assigned and delivered, that no man be so
hardy to hym remove, ne disaray, for any thing that may fall, withoute
commandement of them that hath power, upon peyne of horse and
hernesse to be keped in the conestable warde and mareschal to the
tyme that he hath made fyne with them, also more his body at the
kyng wille.

Every souldeour shal obey his capitaine in all lefulle
thinges, kepe wacche and warde under peyne, &c

6. Also that every man be obeissant to his capitene to kepe his
wacche and warde and forenne, and all that longeth to a souldeour
to doo, upon peyne that his body, horse, and hernes shall be put
undre arrest of the mareschal unto tyme that he that in this offendeth
hat aggreed with his capitene after the warde of the courte.

He that taketh the feithe of a prisoner first shal have him

7. Also be it at battaill or at any other dede of armes, where that
prisonners be take, he that first may have his faith shall have him for
his prisoner, and he shall not nede to abide upon the warde of hym
to the ende of his journey, and noon other shal mow [be allowed to]
take hym, ne have hym for prisoner, but it be founde for his.

No man shall robbe other merchaunt, viteler, surgeon, ne
barbour

8. Also that no man be so hardy to robbe ne spoill other of their
goodes, and namely vitaille, upon peyne of deth. Also that no maner
of man robbe no viteler, marchaunte, leche, surgeone, barbour, ne
no othre man or personne comyng with vitaille for refreisshing of

the ooste upon the same peyne. Ne that no man, souldeour, ne other personne take, robbe, ne pille from other horses meete, ne mannes meete, ne no other thing that is geten of the enemys goods, upon the peyne his body to be arrested at the kinges wille.

No man make debat for armes, prisoners, logyng, under peyne, &c

9. Also that no man debate for armes, prisonners, ne logging, ne for any other thing, so that no riot, contek [dispute], ne debate be in the ooste, ne that no man make hym party in assemblee of people, ne otherwyse, and that as well of principalles as of other parties, upon peyne of losyng of their horses and harnes, till that they have made fyne to the conestable and mareschalle, and their bodyes to be arrested unto the tyme the kynges wille; and yf he be grome or page, he shalle lese his lefte yere. And yf it so be that any man fele hym greved, shew [let him show] his grevaunce to the conestable and mareschall, and he shall have right doone.

No man shall make debat in the ooste for any hate
in tyme passed or to come, under peyne, &c

10. Also that no man be so hardy to make conteke ne debat within the ooste for any hate of tyme passed, ne for to comme, for the which yate, if any man be deede for such contek or debat, he or they that be incheson [occasion] or partyners of the deth, shalbe hanged.

No man escrye his own name, ne his lord, under peyne, &c

11. And yf it happe that any man escrye his own name or the name of his lord or maister, to make a rysing in the people, by the which any affray might fall in the ooste, he that in such wyse escryeth shalbe drawene and hanged.

The peyne of hym that cryeth havok and of them that followeth hym

12. Also that no man be so hardy to cry havok, upon peyne that he that is begynner shal be deede therfore, and the remanent, that doo the same or folow, shal lose their horse and harneis, and the personnes of suche as followeth and escriene shall be under arrest of the conestable and mareschalle warde, unto tyme that they have made fyne and founde suretie no more to offende, and his body in prisone at the kynges wylle.

The peyne of hym that crieth mounte, and the
rewarde of hym that outreth to the conestable

13. Also that no man escrie whiche is called mounte [to ride], nor no
other unreasonable escrie in ooste, upon peyne that he that may be
founde begynner of such an escrie be under arrest of conestable and
mareschalle, and also put from his horse and herneis, unto the tyme
that he hath made a fyne with them, and moreover his body to the
kynges wille of his liffe. And who that certifieth who is begynner,
shal have a hundred shillings for his traveille of the conestable and
mareschalle.

In moustring, no man shew but his own souldeour

14. Also whan it leketh the kyng to take mostre of his ooste, that
no man be so hardy to have any other man at his moustres than thoo
[those] that be with hymself with holden for the hole voyage, withoute fraude, upon peyne to be repreved false and to less alle paiement
that shude be his.

Prisoner

15. Also yf any maner deed of armes be, and any ennemy be borne
to grounde, he that hath born hym so to earth afore, if any other
come after and take his faith, he that taketh his feith shal have the
halfe raunceon of this prisonner, and he that hath hym downe the
other halfe, but he that taketh his feith shalle have the warde of hym,
makyng surete to his partnier.

Prisoner

16. Also if any man take prisoner, and another man comme ypon
hym, askying parte, manassing [menacing] that ellese he will slee
hym, he shal have no parte, thowghe it were so that part had be
graunte unto hym, and yf he slee the prysoner he shalbe arrest of the
conestable and mareschall without deliveraunce, tylle that he have
made gre with the partie, and a fyne after the awarde of the
conestable.

Payement of thirdes

17. Also that every man paye his thirdes to his lord capitene or
maistre of all maner wynnynges of werre, and that also wel, thoo

APPENDIX IV

that be not in wages, as leches, marchaunts, barbours, and other as
other suche as they that be under banner or pennon as of any capitene, upon peyne of losse of his parte of his foresaid wynnyng to this
capitene, and his body to be in warde of the mareschalle, unto he
have his maistre begreed therfore.

*The peyne of hym that reiseth a baner and
called people togidre without licence*

18. Also that no man be so hardy to reyse a baner or a pennon of
Seint George, ne of noon other, to calle and draw togirde and withdraw people oute of the ooste, to goe to any castell, town, or countrey, or any other partie, and that under this peyn, that is to sey,
They that in suche wyse make hemselfe capitans to be draw and
hanged, and they that them sew [sue] and folow to have theire heedes
smyten of, and all theire good and heritage forfeted to the kyng.

19. Also that every man of what estate, nacion, or condition that
he be of, or partie, here a bande of Seint George large, upon the perill
that he wounded or deede in default thereof, he that hym woundeth
or sleeth shal bere no perill ne peyne for his deth. And that no
enemye bere the signe of Seint George, but yf he be a prisoner in the
save warde of his maistre, under peyne of deth therefore.

No man make assault withoute his capiten will it be

20. Also that noon assault be made to castell, ne to strenghe, by
archier ne be other commynes [common soldiers], withoute presence
and will of a speciall assigned [man of estate], under peyne of prisonment. And if any suche assault be made withoute a capitene, after that
proclamation be made by the kyng or conestable and mareschall to
the contrary, that no man be so hardy for to assault after that, and
if any doo it, he shalbe prisoned and lose all other prouffits that he
wanne before the assult, oute take [except] horse and herness for the
werre.

Prisoners and thirdes

21. And if any man take any prisonner, a noon right [as soon be] as
he is taken in the oost, that he bryng his prisoner to his capiten or
maistre, and that upon peyne of lose of his parte to his saide capiten

154

or maistre shal bryng hym within eight dayes to the kyng, conestable, or mareschalle, assoone as he goodly may, so that he be no other way, upon peyne to lose his parte to hym to be yeven, that shal yeve to the conestable and mareschall first warnyng thereof. And that every man kepe or doo kepe his prisoner, that he rede not at large in hostyeng, ne goo at large in loggyng, but yf a wayte be hadde upon hym, upon payne to loose his prisonner, reservyng to his maistre or lorde his thirde of the hole, yf he be not partyner of the default, and the second parte to hym that shalle mowe first fynde hym [shall first accuse him] and the thirde parte to the conestable, and upon the same peyne, and also more over his body in arrest to the kyng wille, that he suffre not his prisoner to go out of the oost for his raunson, ne for no other cause without save-conduit.

Watche and warde shalbe keped

22. And that every man bysily by provision of the mareschall kepe duely watche in the ooste, and that with as many men of arms and archiers as to hym shall be assigned, but yf he have a cause reasonable approved before the conestable and mareschalle, and therto that he abyde the terme to hym lymited, not departyng from thens away but by assignement and licence, upon peyn of smytyng of his heede that departed otherwyse.

No man graunte save-conduit, nor breek hit, under peyn, &c

23. Also that no man yeve save-conduit to prisoner, ne to no other, nother licence to no enemye to comme ne goo oute in to the oost, upon peyne to forfed all his good to the kyng, and his body in arreste at kyng wille, except our lorde the kyng, conestable, and mareschall. And that no man be so hardy to breke the kyng saveconduit, upon peyn to be drawn and hanged, and his good and heritages to be forfed to the kyng, nother of the conestable and mareschal save-conduit upon peyne of dethe.

No man shal take ne wit-holde any mannes servaunt waged

24. Also that no man be so hardy to take or witholde servaunt of any other, the whiche is a covenaunt for the viage, that is to say, souldeour, man of armes, archier, groom, or page, after tyme that he is asked or challenged by his maistre, upon this peyne, his body

to be arrested unto tyme he make gree unto the party complanaunt after the warde of the courte, and his horse and his harneis forfed to the conestable tyll he have made his fyne.

The peyne of hym that departeth from the oos without licence of his capiten

25. Also that no man be so hardy to departe from the stale withoute leve or licence of his lord or maistre, upon peyne that the body of hym that otherwyse departeth be in arrest at the kyng wille, and in peyne of lesing of all his wynnyng that day, reserved to his lord or maistre the thirde of his wynnyng, and to the lord of the stale all that he hath departed shall wynne that day and so fro day to day, that this ordenaunce be befild.

If any escrye be made every man shall draw him to the cheif capitene

26. Also yf any escrie fall in the oost whan it is logged, that every man draw to the kyng or to the cheiftane of the batelle, levying keped his loggyng sufficiently, but yf the enemie falle in that syde where he is logged, and in this case the said capiten shall abyde therin hymself and alle his menne.

No man be so hardy to robbe a countrey wonne after proclamacion be made

27. And if any countrey or lordship be wonne other by free wille offred to the kynges obeisaunce, that no man be so hardy to robbe ne pille them, after the peas be proclamed, upon peyne of deth. And if any man of what degree, so he be comme to our said lord obeissaunce, that no man take hym, robbe, ne pille hym, ypon the same peyne, so that he or they that thus will obey bere a token of our souverain lord the kynge.

No man shal selle his prisoner, nor make fynaunce, without licence of his capitene

28. Also that no man be so hardy to raunsone or selle his prisoner withoute especialle licence of his capitene, which entendeth with [has an indenture with] the kyng undre his lettre and sealle, and that on payn that he that doeth the contrary therof fforfete his parte in the

prisoner to his capitene, and he to be under arrest of the mareschal
unto the tyme that he have made agrement to his capiten. And that
no man bye such a prysoner, upon peyne to lose his money that he
paid for hym, and the prisoner to be restored to the capiten above-
said.

No man brenne without commandement

29. Also that withoute especial commaundement of the kyng no
man brenne, upon peyen of deth.

Watche shall be by day and night in loggynges

30. Also both day and night every man have watch within his
loggyng, upon peyn of arrest of his body tyll he have made fyne and
raunson with the kyng at the kyng will.

Every man shall enjoy as moche vitaill as he findeth, and as moche as he needeth, and the remanent departe with the oost

31. Also yf any man fynde vyne or any other vitaill, that he take hym-
selfe therof as moche as hym needeth, and that he save the remanent
to other of the ooste withoute destruction, upon peyn his horse and
harness to be arrest till he have made fyne with the conestable.

No man make roode withoute licence

32. Also that no man make no ridyng by day ne by night but by
licence and knowleche of the chevestens [chieftains] of the battaille,
so that the chevesten may know what way they draw theime, and
that they may have socour and helpe, if nede be, upon peyn of them
that offendeth of their bodyes and good to the kyng wille.

33. Also that the capiten of no warde graunte no roode without
licence of the kyng.

No man breke no array ne goo of the ooste withoute licence

34. And also that for no tything, ne no maner estrie that may come
into the ooste, no man moeve hym in disarray of the bataill, yf they
ridenne, but by leve of the chevestens of the bataille, upon peyn that
he had offended shal be put from his horse and harneis to the warde
of the conestable and mareschall, unto that he hath made fyne with
them, and fynde suretie that he shall no more offende.

APPENDIX IV

Every man shalle have the copie of thordenaunce, and proclamation shall be made

Also that these poynt afore writene whiche be needful are to be cryed in the ooste, and also it is nedefull that the copie be yeven to every governour of men in the ooste, so that they may have playne knowlech to enforme their men of the forsaide ordenaunce.

[These ordinances, which are believed to be a translation of a Latin version of the King's statutes 'to be keped in time of werre', were printed in *The Blacke Booke of the Admiralty*.]

King Henry V's Challenge
to the Dauphin

Henry by the grace of God King of England and of France, and Lord of Ireland, to the high and puissant Prince, the Dauphin of Vienne, our Cousin, eldest son of the most puissant Prince, our Cousin and Adversary of France. From the reverence of God, and to avoid the effusion of human blood, We have many times, and in many ways, sought peace, and notwithstanding that We have not been able to attain it, our desire to possess it increases more and more. And well considering that the effect of our wars are the deaths of men, destruction of countries, lamentations of women and children, and so many general evils that every good christian must lament it and have pity, and We especially, whom this matter more concerns, We are induced to seek diligently for all possible means to avoid the above-mentioned evils, and to acquire the approbation of God, and the praise of the world.

Whereas We have considered and reflected, that as it hath pleased God to visit our said Cousin your Father, with infirmity, with Us and You lie the remedy, and to the end that every one may know that We do not prevent it, We offer to place our quarrel, at the will of God, between Our Person and Yours. And if it should appear to you that you cannot accept this offer on account of the interest which you think our said Cousin your Father has in it, We declare to you that if you are willing to accept it and to do what we propose, it pleases us to permit that our said Cousin, from the reverence of God and that he is a sacred person, shall enjoy that which he at present has for the term of his life, whatever it may please God shall happen between Us and You, as it shall be agreed between his council, ours and yours. Thus, if God shall give us the victory, the crown of France with its appurtenances as our right, shall be immediately rendered to us without difficulty, after his decease, and that to this all the lords and estates of the kingdom of France shall be bound in manner as shall be agreed between us. For it is better for us, Cousin, to decide this war for ever between our two persons, than to suffer the unbelievers by means of our quarrels to destroy Christianity, our mother the Holy Church to remain in division, and the people of God to destroy one another. We pray that you may have such anxious desire to it, and to seek for peace, that you will neglect no means by which it can be obtained. Let us hope in God that a better or shorter way of effecting it cannot be found; and therefore in discharge of our soul, and in charge of yours, if great evils follow, we propose to you what is above said. Protesting that we make this our offer to the honor and fear of God, and for the reasons above mentioned, of our own motion without our loyal relations, counsellors, and subjects now around us, having in so high a matter dared to advise us; nor can it at any time to come be urged to our prejudice, nor in prejudice of our good right and title which We have at present to the said crown with its appurtenances; nor to the good right and title which We now have to other lands and heritages on this side the sea; nor to our heirs and successors, if this our offer does not take full effect between Us and You, in the manner above said. Given under our Privy Seal, at our town of Harfleur, the xvi day of September.

[From Thomas Rymer's *Foedera, Conventiones, Literae et cujuscunque generis Acta Publica inter Reges Angliae*, ix (1709), and translated in Sir Harris Nicolas's *History of the Battle of Agincourt* (1832).]

NOTE ON SOURCES

KEY TO LETTERS IN TEXT

[A] *Henrici Quinti Angliae Regis Gesta* (B.M. Cotton MS. Julius E. IV; ed. Williams).

[B] *Titi Livii Foro* (Cambridge University, Corpus Christi MS. N. 31; ed. Hearne).

[C] Jean Juvenal des Ursins (Bibliothèque Nationale).

[D] *Chronique de Jean Le Fèvre de St Remy* (Boulogne-sur-Mer MS. 150; ed. Morland).

[E] *Thomas de Eltham vita et Gesta* (Coll. Arms, Arundel MS.; ed. Hearne).

[F] *The Chronicle of John Hardyng* (B.M. Lansdowne MS. 204; ed. Ellis).

[G] *Chronique de Enguerrand de Monstrelet* (Bibliothèque Nationale MS. 8347; ed. Douët-d'Arcq).

[H] *Chronique de Religieux de Saint-Denys* (Bibliothèque Nationale MS. 5958; ed. Bellaguet).

For a battle fought 550 years ago Agincourt is extremely well documented. There are several contemporary sources and some eye-witness accounts from both sides. These sources are listed in the bibliography and marked with an asterisk.

Of the English accounts the best is *Henrici Quinti Angliae Regis Gesta*. This was written within two years by one of the priests of the King's chapel who watched the battle from the baggage park, which was much closer to the fighting than was usual. This priest is supposed, on no very sure authority, to be Thomas Elmham, the Cluniac Prior of Lenton, whose *Liber Metricus de Henrico Quinto* was edited by C. A. Cole in 1858. He is not the author of *Vita et Gesta Henrici Quinti Anglorum Regis,* though this work was attributed to him by Thomas Hearne, the antiquary, who edited it in 1727.

Titi Livii Foro—Juliensis Vita Henrici Quinti is by Henry V's Italian biographer, Tito Livio of Forlì, who came to England as the Duke of Gloucester's 'poet and orator' in about 1436. Much of his information is based on *The Brut* and on Monstrelet; but much else obviously came from his patron, who wanted to cut a good figure in the biography of his brother that he had commissioned. The English translation of Tito Livio's work done in 1513 contains additional material derived from the Ormonde family. James Butler, the 4th Earl, served in the Agincourt campaign.

Thomas Walsingham's *Historia Anglicana* is based also on second-hand information though it was written within three years of the campaign. John Hardyng and Jean Le Fèvre, Lord of St Remy, however, both served in the Agincourt campaign on the English side, John Hardyng in the retinue of Sir Robert Umphraville, Le Fèvre as a nineteen-year-old pursuivant-at-arms.

Two of the chronicles from the French side, Jean de Waurin's and Enguerrand de Monstrelet's, bear a strong resemblance to Le Fèvre's. Jean de Waurin served with his father in the French army as a boy of fifteen and, like Le Fèvre, wrote his account many years later, after comparing notes—or so it seems—with his former enemy. De Monstrelet did not serve in the campaign but was born near Agincourt. His chronicle appeared within twenty-five years of the battle, which was earlier than either Le Fèvre's or de Waurin's. The best of the French accounts is the one by the Saint-Denis monk. Although the official Orleanist history, it contains little of the prejudice and misrepresentation which mars the history of Jean Juvenal des Ursins.

Several of these sources were collected together by Sir Harris Nicolas, whose *History of the Battle of Agincourt* was published in 1833. This remains the most detailed account in English, though Sir James Ramsay's *Lancaster and York* (1892) and J. H. Wylie's *The Reign of Henry V* (1919) both contain additional material and A. H. Burne's *The Agincourt War: A Military History of the latter part of the Hundred Years War from 1369 to 1453* (1956) contains far more analysis. Colonel Burne's is an admirable book—though the maps are scarcely decipherable—but I have not always found the application of his test of 'Inherent Military Probability' convincing, and I have differed from him in interpreting and reconciling various contradictory statements in the chronicles. This is, no doubt, inevitable and I do not pretend that I have proved his interpretations and assumptions to be wrong or mine to be right.

The best of the modern biographies of Henry V are, I think, C. L. Kingsford's, R. B. Mowat's, Margaret Wade Labarge's, and Harold

F. Hutchinson's important recent study. Peter Earle's and C. T. Allmand's are good shorter accounts.

Modern scholarly studies of the mediaeval military organisation the King inherited and adapted have been written for the specialist by R. A. Newhall, Herbert James Hewitt, Maurice Hugh Keen and Michael Powicke. Theirs are excellent books. It may be thought, though, that the claims made for Henry V as a strategist in *The English Conquest of Normandy, 1416–1424* are somewhat extravagant.

The background of the Hundred Years War has been well described recently by G. A. Holmes, V. H. H. Green, Kenneth Fowler and A. R. Myers, and in greater detail by E. F. Jacob in *Henry V and the Invasion of France* (1947) and *The Fifteenth Century* (1961).

The most thorough French account is René de Belleval's, published in 1862. Ferdinand Lot's attempt to show that the English outnumbered the French in the battle has not been found acceptable by other historians; and Edouard Perroy's *La Guerre de Cent Ans* does not concern itself with military details.

Almost all the sources for the Agincourt campaign have been printed though not all have been translated into English. The Public Record Office papers contain lists of retinues and the Muster Rolls of the army at Southampton (E 101/51/2) and at Harfleur (E 101/48/19). A list of commanders and the numbers of their retinues was compiled from such sources in 1850 by Joseph Hunter in his *Critical and Historical Tracts* (No. 1).

BIBLIOGRAPHY

ALLMAND, C. T.: *Henry V* (Historical Association, 1968).

BELLAGUET, L. (ed.): *La Chronique de Religieux de Saint-Denys, contenant le règne de Charles VI de 1380–1422* (1839–1852).

BELLEVAL, Réne de: *La Grande Guerre* (1862).

BLAIR, Claude: *European Armour* (B. T. Batsford, Ltd., 1958). *European and American Arms, c. 1100–1850* (B. T. Batsford, Ltd., 1962).

*BRIE, F. W. (ed.): *The Brut, or the Chronicles of England* (1908).

BURNE, Lieutenant-Colonel Alfred H.: *The Agincourt War: A Military History of the Hundred Years War from 1369 to 1453* (Eyre and Spottiswoode, 1956). 'Lessons from Agincourt', *The Army Quarterly* (April 1951).

CHAMBERLIN, E. R.: *The Hundred Years War: the English in France, 1337–1453* (Constable, 1978).

CHURCH, A. J.: *Henry V* (1889).

CLOWES, W. L.: *The Royal Navy*, Vol. 1 (1897).

*COLE, Charles Augustus (ed.): *Memorials of Henry V King of England: Vita Henrici Quinti* (Redmayne); *Versus Rhythmici in Laudem Henrici Quinti; Liber Metricus de Henrico Quinto* (Elmham) (1858).

DAVIES, J. D. Griffith: *Henry V* (1935).

*DOUËT- D'ARCQ, L.: *La Chronique de Enguerrand de Monstrelet, 1400–1444* (1857–1862).

EARLE, Peter: *The Life and Times of Henry V* (Weidenfeld & Nicolson, 1972).

*ELLIS, Henry (ed.): *The Chronicle of John Hardyng* (1812).

EMMERIG, Oskar: 'The Bataille of Agyncourt' in Lichte geschichtlicher Quellenwerke* (1906).

FORTESCUE, Hon. J. W.: *A History of the British Army*, Vol. 1 (1899).

FOWLER, Kenneth: *The Hundred Years War* (Macmillan, 1971).

*GALBRAITH V. H. (ed.): *The St. Alban's Chronicle, 1406–1420, by Thomas Walsingham* (1937).

Gesta Henrici Quinti. The Deeds of Henry the Fifth. Translated from the Latin with introduction and notes by F. Taylor and John S. Roskell (Oxford, 1975).

GREEN, V. H. H.: *The Later Plantagenets* (Edward Arnold, Ltd., 1955).

BIBLIOGRAPHY

*HARDY, William (ed.): *Recueil des Croniques et Anchiennes Istories de la Grant Bretaigne par Jehan de Waurin* (1868).

HAY, D.: 'The Divisions of the Spoils of War', R.H.S. Trans., 5th Series, iv (1954).

*HEARNE, Thomas (ed.): *Thomas de Elmham Vita et Gesta Henrici Quinti Anglorum Regis* (1727). *Titi Livii Foro—Juliensis Vita Henrici Quinti* (1716).

HEWITT, Herbert James: *The Organisation of War under Edward III, 1338-62* (Manchester University Press, 1966).

Histoire de Charles VI, Roy de France, escrite par les Ordres et sur les Memoires et les Avis de Guy de Monceaux et de Philippe de Villette . . . Traduite sur le manuscrit latin . . . par M. le Laboureur (1663).

HOLMES, George: *The Later Middle Ages, 1272–1485* (Thomas Nelson & Sons Ltd., 1962).

HUNTER, Joseph: *Critical and Historical Tracts* (No. 1)—*A Contribution Towards an authentic list of the Commanders of the English Host in King Henry V's Expedition to France* (1850).

HUTCHINSON, Harold F.: *Henry V: A Biography* (Eyre and Spottiswoode, 1967).

JACOB, E. F.: *Henry V and the Invasion of France* (Hodder and Stoughton, 1947). *The Fifteenth Century, 1399–1485* (Oxford University Press, 1961).

KEEN, Maurice Hugh: *The Laws of War in the Late Middle Ages* (Routledge and Kegan Paul, 1965).

KINGSFORD, Charles Lethbridge: *English Historical Literature in the Fifteenth Century* (1913). *Henry V: The Typical Medieval Hero* (2nd edition, 1923). (Ed.): *The First English Life of King Henry V written in 1513 by an anonymous author known commonly as 'The Translator of Livius'* (1911).

LABARGE, Margaret Wade: *Henry V: The Cautious Conqueror* (Eyre and Spottiswoode, 1975).

LEFEVRE, Raymonde: *Le Cinquième Henry* (1967).

LINDSAY, Philip: *King Henry V: A Chronicle* (1934).

LOT, Ferdinand: *L'Art Militaire et les Armées en Moyen Âge en Europe* (1946).

LUARD, Lt. Col. John: *A History of the Dress of the British Soldier* (1852).

MAZAS, Alexandre: *Vies des Grands Capitaines Français de Moyen Âge*, Vol. 6 (1829).

*MORLAND, F. (ed.): *Chronique de Jean Le Fèvre de St. Remy, 1408–1435* (1876–1881).

MORRIS, J. E.: 'Mounted Infantry in Medieval Warfare', R.H.S. Trans., 3rd Series, viii (1914).

MOWAT, R. B.: *Henry the Fifth* (1919).

MYERS, A. R.: *England in the Later Middle Ages* (1952).

NEWHALL, Richard Ager: *The English Conquest of Normandy, 1416–1424* (1924). *Muster and Review: A Problem of English Military Administration* (Harvard University Press, 1940).

NICOLAS, Sir Harris: *History of the Battle of Agincourt and of the Expedition of Henry the Fifth into France in 1415* (1833).

OMAN, Sir Charles: *A History of the Art of War in the Middle Ages*, Vol. 2 (1924). *The Art of War in the Middle Ages 1378–1515* (revised and edited by John H. Beeler) (Cornell University Press, 1953).

OTTERBOURNE, Thomas: *Duo Rerum Anglicarum* (1732).

PALMER, J. J. N.: *England, France and Christendom, 1377-99* (Routledge and Kegan Paul, 1972).

PERROY, Edouard: *La Guerre de Cent Ans* (Gallimard, 1945).

*PETITOT, M. (ed.): *Mémoires de Pierre de Fenin, Escuyer et Panetier de Charles VI Roy de France* (1825).

POWICKE, Michael: *Military Obligation in Mediaeval England: A Study in Liberty and Duty* (Oxford University Press, 1962).

PRINCE, A. E.: 'The Indenture System under Edward III' in *Historical Essays Presented to J. Tait* (ed. J. G. Edwards) (1931). 'The Payment of Army Wages', *Spectrum*, xiv (1944).

PUBLIC RECORD OFFICE PAPERS: E101/46/24; E101/51/2; E101/48/19; E101/47/20.

RAMSAY, Sir James H.: *Lancaster and York, 1399–1485* (1892).

*RILEY, H. T. (ed.): *Historia Anglicana by Thomas Walsingham* (1864).

RYMER, Thomas: *Foedera, Conventiones, Literae et cujuscunque generis Acta Publica inter Reges Angliae*, Vol. ix (1709).

SMAIL, R. C.: 'The Art of War', Vol. 1, *Medieval England* (ed. Austin Lane Poole, Oxford University Press, 1958).

*TAYLOR, Frank (ed.): *Chronicle of John Strecche for the Reign of Henry V, 1414–1422* (1932).

THOMPSON, Peter E. (Ed.): *Contemporary Chronicles of the Hundred Years War* (Folio Society, 1966).

*TUETEY, Alexandre (ed.): *Journal d'un Bourgeois de Paris, 1405–1449* (1881).

TWISS, Sir Travers (ed.): *The Blacke Booke of the Admiralty*, Vol. 1 (1871).

TYLER, J. Endell: *Henry of Monmouth* (1838).

*URSINS, Jean Juvenal des: *Histoire du Roy Charles VI* (1653).

BIBLIOGRAPHY

VALE, M. G. A.: *English Gascony, 1399-1453* (Oxford University Press, 1970).

VICKERS, Kenneth H.: *England in the Later Middle Ages* (4th edition, 1926). *Humphrey, Duke of Gloucester* (1907).

*WILLIAMS, Benjamin (ed.): *Henrici Quinti Angliae Regis Gesta* (1850).

WYLIE, James Hamilton: *The Reign of Henry the Fifth*, Vol. 2 (1415–1416) (1919). 'Notes on the Agincourt Roll', *R.H.S. Trans.*, 3rd Series, v (1911).

INDEX

The numerals in **heavy type** refer to the *figure numbers* of the black and white illustrations (between pages 80 and 81)

INDEX

Boucicaut—*continued*
  ford at Blanche-Taque guarded by his
    force, 80
  favours Fabian tactics; probable move-
    ments; on the north bank of the Somme,
    82
  joins the main body of the army, 88
  aware of the dangers of fighting in out-
    moded style, 98
  in front line, 101
  advises waiting, 104
  captured, 115
  a prisoner, 121
  dies in England, 127
Boulogne, 46
Bourbon, Louis, 2nd Duke of,
  adheres to Orléanist cause, 22
  withdraws support for French cause, 66
  reconsiders decision, 81
  sends heralds to challenge Henry V, 88
  in front line, 101
  captured, 115
  life spared, 116
  a prisoner, 121
  dies in England, 127
Bournonville, Ganiot de, 113
Boves, 83, 84
Bowmen (*see also* Archers), 98, 110, 111
  cross-bowmen, 35, 82
  cut stakes, 85
  ford the Somme, 86
  French bowmen, 114
  French cross-bowmen, 101, 110
  long-bowmen, 35, 110
Bows (*see also* Weapons), 29, 86, 111
  bowstaves, 28
  bow-strings, 105, 109
  construction and use, 35
  cross-bow, 36, 54, 56
  long-bow, 36, 37
  short-bow, 36
Brabant, Duke of, 115, 121
  promises to join the army, 82
  rallies his supporters, 114
  killed, 116-117
Braquemont, Lionel de, 67
Bresle, River, 79, 80, 138
Brétigny, Treaty of (1346), 20, 21, 22
Bretons, 115
Bridgehead, 86, 87
Bridges, 75
  across the moat at Harfleur, 56, 60
  at Abbeville, 83
  at Arques, 79
  at Corbie, 84
  at Frévent, 90
  London Bridge, 131
Bristol, 37
Brittany, 20
Brittany, Duke of, 22, 81
Burgundians, 66, 115
Burgundy, 21, 66, 137
Burgundy, John the Fearless, Duke of
  (1371-1419), 82, 114, 137; **16**
  effect on France of his quarrels with
    Duke of Orléans, 21
  Henry V needs his friendship, 22
  his devious behaviour, 66
  equivocation, 72

Earl of Arundel fears his power, 73
Burgundy, Philip the Bold, Duke of (1342-
  1404), 20, 21
Burne, Lt.-Col. Alfred H., 99, 117, 137, 162

Caen, 139
Calais, 20, 46, 67, 68, 72, 73, 74, 80, 81, 83,
  84, 85, 87, 88, 89, 96, 124, 126, 127,
  128, 137, 138
  Calais Pale, 38, 72, 127
  Calais road, 92, 117, 138
Cambridge, Richard, Earl of (*d.* 1460), 44
Camoys, Lord, 101, 125, 136
Canche, River, 91
Canterbury Cathedral, 131
Castle, Sir John, 44
Catherine of Valois (1401-1437), 22, 40,
  139; **28**
Cavalry, 29, 36, 53, 85; **21**
  French cavalry, 80, 101, 109-110
  lancers, 81
Challenge, 32, 70, 82, 88, 105, 138
  Henry's Challenge to the Dauphin, 159
Champagne, 82
Chaplains (*see also* Priests), 32, 33, 52, 64,
  77, 90, 104, 126, 139, 149
Charles V of France (1337-1380), 20, 21
Charles VI of France (1368-1422), 20, 54,
  66, 70, 72, 88, 105, 122
  marriage; madness, 21
  receives letters from Henry V, 39, 40
  replies to Henry's letters, 65
Charolais, Philip, Count of (son of John the
  Fearless, Duke of Burgundy), 66
Chaulnes, 85
Cheapside, 133
Chef de Caux, 47
Chevauchée, 70, 71, 137
Chevaux de Frise, 85
Chivalry, 26, 32, 34, 98, 132, 135
Chroniclers, 40, 79, 81, 92, 96, 99, 104, 124,
  161-162
  French chroniclers, 77, 79, 101, 114, 117
Cinque Ports, 28, 59, 128
  Barons of, 128
Citizens, 28
  of Calais, 126
  of London, 131
  of Paris, 82
Clarence, Thomas, Duke of (*c.* 1388-1421),
  47, 59, 64; **6**
  contract with the King, 31
  takes a detachment hard by Harfleur, 51
  moves further out of Harfleur, 53
  captures wagons and equipment, 54
  contracts dysentery, 65
  sent home sick, 69
Clerks, 30, 32, 52
Cologne, River, 89
Commissions of array, 29
Confession, 92, 95, 98
Confessor, Henry's, 139
Corbie, 84, 85
Cornhill, 133
Cornwall, Sir John, 136
  goes ashore at Harfleur, 48
  with Sir Gilbert Umfraville commands
    the vanguard leaving Harfleur, 77
  leads vanguard at Somme crossing, 87

INDEX

INDEX

Roos, Lord de, 77
Rouen, 54, 65, 69, 71, 73, 82, 88, 138, 139
  siege of, 135
Ruisseauville, 123

Sacrament, 53, 102, 106, 127, 135
Sailors, 45, 63
  impress of, 37
Saint-Aubin-de-Cretot, 68
Saint Denis, 47, 110
  Cathedral of, 65
St George, 43, 81, 106
  cross of, 53
  statue of, 132
  vision of, 122
St-Omer, 66
St Paul's, 45, 128, 133, 134
St Pol, Count of, 90
St Thomas of Canterbury (Becket, *c.* 1118-
    1170), 19
  shrine, 131
Sandwich, 37, 126
Scouts, 81, 83, 86, 88, 91, 138
  French scouts, 83
Scrope, Lord (King's Treasurer), 44
Seals, King's, 77; **26**
Siege-train, 55, 58, 60, 63; **10**
  battering rams, 28, 56
  catapults, 58
  ladders, 64
  levers, 57
  mines, 56
  scaling-ladders, 28
  screens, 57
  siege-equipment, 51, 58
  spade, 56
Seine, River, 46, 54, 69, 82
  estuary, 46, 47, 56, 59, 66
  valley, 46, 52, 59
Sergeant-at-Arms, 37
Shakespeare, 96, 135
Sheriffs, 38
Ships, 28, 37, 126; **4, 5**
  barges, 28
  boats, 56
  catch fire, 45
  masters of, 28, 37
  master of the *Trinité Royale*, 43
  pavises, 43
  ship-repairing, 47
  the *Catherine*, 69
  the *Holy Ghost*, 69
  the *Katherine de la Tour*, 43
  the King's ship, 120
  the *Petite Trinité de la Tour*, 43
  the *Rude Coq de la Tour*, 43
  the *Trinité Royale*, 43, 45, 46, 47, 69
Sigismund, Emperor, German King and
    Roman Emperor (1368-1437), 40
Sluys, 46
Soissons, 64
Solent, 28, 43, 69
Somme, River, 73, 75, 80, 82, 85, 86, 87, 88,
    91, 137, 138
  Somme valley, 80, 81
Southampton, 37, 40, 69
Southwark, 131
Spithead, 43

Standards (*see also* Banners), 43, 131, 133
  ensigns, 43
  pennons, 45, 96
  Royal Standard, 132
Statute of Winchester (1285), 29
Suffocation, 112, 121
Suffolk, Michael de la Pole, second earl of,
    54, 121; **7**
  occupies position near Harfleur, 51
  contracts dysentery, 58
  dies, 65
Suffolk, third earl of,
  killed at Agincourt, 121
  bones taken to England, 123
Supplies, 45, 72, 74
  coal, 69
  equipment, 28, 45
  cords, 28
  glue, 69
  ropes, 57, 69
  stores, 51, 69, 82, 96
  royal stores, 58
  tar, 57
  tools, 28
  torches, 64
Surgeons, 32, 52, 147
Sword, 29, 34, 99, 106, 111, 115
  Henry's sword, 102; and helmet, **23, 24**
  sword-belt, 33
  sword of state, 77

Taxes, 25, 27
Tents, 67, 133
  pavilions, 67, 134
  royal tents, 52, 86
Ternoise, River, 91
Thames, River, 37
Tower of London, 37, 127
Tower (of Harfleur), 47, 57
Trades:
  dyeing, 47
  weaving, 47
  wool, 21
Tradesmen, 30, 32, 68
  armourers, 32, 95, 147
  artisans, 69, 82
  bowyers, 32, 35, 37, 148
  carpenters, 32, 37, 44, 52, 57, 148
  carters, 32
  cartwrights, 37
  colliers, 148
  cordeners, 32, 148
  craftsmen, 131
  farriers, 32
  fletchers, 32, 148
  grooms, 32, 33, 52, 82, 147
  labourers, 37, 57, 147, 149
  masons, 32, 37, 43, 69
  painters, 32, 52, 147
  pavilioners, 52, 147
  purveyors, 32
  saddlers, 32, 147
  smiths, 32, 37
  tentmakers, 32
  tilemakers, 69
  turners, 32, 38
  wheelwrights, 32, 37, 148

INDEX

Tramecourt, 92, 98, 109
  Marchioness of, 123
Transport, 30
  carts, 37, 53, 72, 74, 77, 86, 87, 96
  pack animals, 72, 77, 86
  Sergeant of the Wagons, 37
  wagons, 28, 54, 138
Treasurer, King's, *see under* Scrope, Lord
Trial by peers, 44
Troyes, Treaty of (1420), 139
Truce, 64, 66

Umfraville, Sir Gilbert, 136
  goes ashore at Harfleur, 48
  bears the King's helmet and crown, 67
  with Sir John Cornwall commands the
    vanguard leaving Harfleur, 77
  crosses the Somme, 87
Umphraville, Sir Robert, 162

Vendôme, Count of, 121
Verney, Henry, 69
Vernon, 64, 65, 66, 72, 73
Vincennes, 139
Voyennes, 86, 87, 88, 138

Wages, 25, 28, 29, 30, 31
  scales of payment, 32
Wars of the Roses, 25
Warwick, Earl of, Captain of Calais, 48, 138
  escorts the King into Calais, 126
Weapons, 28, 29, 34, 45, 77, 103, 104, 111,
    114, 122
  arrows, 28, 29, 35, 54, 59, 63, 84, 95, 98,

  101, 106, 109, 110, 111
  axes, 34, 99, 111, 134
    battle-axe, 113, 131
    pole-axe, 33
  bill-hooks, 111
  clubs, 106, 109
  daggers, 34
  halberds, 111, 133
  hatchets, 111
  knives, 29
  lances, 34, 101, 104, 111
  maces, 111
  quivers, 29
  spears, 114
Westminster, 38
  Abbey, 19
Westmorland, Earl of, 48
Whittington, Richard (d. 1423), 28
Wight, Isle of, 26, 43
William I, the Conqueror (1027/8-1087), 20,
    46
Winchelsea, 37, 69
Windsor, 127
Wounded, 64, 116, 121, 123
Wvlie, Dr J. H., 137, 162

York, Duke of (1373-1415), 44, 47
  leads the rearguard out of Harfleur, 77
  suggests the bowmen cut stakes, 85
  takes the French heralds to the King, 88
  commands the right at Agincourt, 101
  dead from suffocation, 121
  bones taken to England, 123

Zierickzee, 127

176